REINHAR BONNKL

HELL EMPTY HEAVEN FULL

FULFILLING THE MISSION

PART TWO

HELL EMPTY HEAVEN FULL

Part II

Fulfilling the Mission

Reinhard Bonnke
with George Canty

… before me was a great multitude that no one could count,
from every nation, tribe, people and language,
standing before the throne and in front of the Lamb …
And they cried out in a loud voice:
"Salvation belongs to our God,
who sits on the throne, and to the Lamb."
Revelation 7:9-10

HELL EMPTY HEAVEN FULL
Part II
Fulfilling the Mission

Reinhard Bonnke with George Canty
English

Copyright © E-R Productions LLC 2006
ISBN 1-933106-57-3

Edition 1, Printing 1
5,000 copies

Cover Design: Brand Navigation, U.S.A.
Typeset: Roland Senkel
Photographs by: Rob Birkbeck
Oleksandr Volyk
Robert Russell
Mark Theisinger
Roland Senkel

E-R Productions LLC
P.O. Box 593647
Orlando, Florida 32859
U.S.A.

www.e-r-productions.com

Printed in Singapore by PH Productions Pte Ltd

Contents

In evangelism there is no "right" way of doing things, only right principles, principles that can be drawn from the New Testament. The apostle Paul himself said, "That I might by all means save some." The test of what is "right" is whether the Holy Spirit makes it his chariot.

It is unfortunate that certain methods seem to become sacrosanct. We can fight with one another over traditions which may actually be non-functional; the machine itself becomes more greatly admired than the product. Being faithful and being a stick-in-the-mud are not the same thing. Christian faithfulness means being faithful to Christ's message. Circumstances may call for a new or radical approach but the fundamental objective is to reach people everywhere with the message of salvation and to touch them with the finger of Christ's love.

I am amazed by the brilliance of thought in the world church today. At the same time, brilliance may be an intellectual exercise on the periphery of life as opposed to hard work in the harvest field. Sadly, so much mental effort goes into doctrinal quibbles, technical irrelevancies and exercises in philosophical debate. If we are to go all out to "save some", it is, of course, legitimate to think about how we are going to do it. Genius is welcome and has a worthy subject in the Gospel. The problem is if it stops there.

There are 32 chapters in this two-volume work. It was originally planned as a single volume but the material quickly became enough for two because there are so many matters vitally linked to the proclamation of the Gospel of Christ. That is what I have learned in more than 30 years of devotion to the single purpose of bringing men and women into the Kingdom of God. Doing the work can be far more satisfying if we understand what we are really doing – measuring our activities against the standards set by the Word itself. Knowing the Word in the way taught in these chapters also means great efficiency. Psalm 1 promises "whatever he does prospers". Who is the psalmist talking about? The previous verses have already identified him – the man who meditates on the Word.

Praying is important and fulfils many purposes, but nowhere does Scripture promise triumphs of evangelism and success in outreach as a result of prayer alone. The key is the Word. God instructed Joshua, *"Do not let this Book of the Law depart from your mouth; meditate on it day and night, so that you may be careful to do everything written in it. Then you will be prosperous and successful"* (Joshua 1:8).

Demanding of God that he step in and do the work, perhaps fasting as if to put him under an obligation, finds no encouragement in the Word. The Word cries out to be heard. *"Hear me, you who know what is right"* (Isaiah 51:7). The Word wants to be known and wants to be passed on; it needs people who are living seeds of the Word. The Word is the secret of an evangelist's success.

I have tried in these two volumes to do justice to the counsel God saw fit to leave in the Word, this treasure in a field. We have crossed the whole field of evangelism searching to find out where the needs lay and then endeavouring to bring counsel by the words of the Word. One of my basic aims, founded on the Word, is to set believers on their way, staff in hand, to turn the world upside down for Christ, for God so loved the world. That makes the Gospel a global business. Scripture never suggests anything different.

Evangelist Reinhard Bonnke
Author

Part 1

By my God I can scale a wall.

2 Samuel 22:30

CHAPTER 1

That Superman?

"The Spirit told me to go."
Acts 11:12 NKJV

Someone said that the world has yet to see what God will do with a man wholly surrendered to his will. This popular quote is a criticism of everybody who has ever served God. In fact, countless men and women have been wholly surrendered. Their surrender is not to be judged by their visible achievements. Martyrs have died fully surrendered without achieving much. The Romans beheaded a dedicated Christian girl who was only 13 years old.

According to some, "the man God uses" would be a paragon of virtues: a man of prayer, a man of the word, a man of faith, a man of integrity, dedicated, faithful, patient, loving, separated from the world. Sermons add quality after quality to the qualifications that are said to be needed. Would anybody have time to be all they are supposed to be? With the perfect wife of Proverbs 27 they would need a 48-hour day.

When I was young, I read books on Christian heroes, men and women who had done daring things for God, fought battles, and wrought victories. The stories all spoke of their flawless saintliness and greatness. I revered them all and still treasure what I learned about them but I began to suspect that all great men were dead, that *"there were giants on the earth in those days"* (Genesis 6:4 NKJV) but that nobody was born like that today. Reading about "perfect" people can be dismally discouraging after a while.

The life stories of great Christians are now being re-written. A more rounded style is showing other sides of their character. The old-style glowing hagiographies are being reshaped as biographies of flesh and blood beings, not semi-gods. Everyone is human and, knowing our limitations, it is helpful to find that past exploits were performed by people who had not attained angelic perfection. Jesus said, *"No one is good"* (Luke 18:19). How right he was! The earthly state of even the best of God's children is not flawless. If God could use only impeccable characters, there would be nobody to do the work and it would never get done.

We must still understand that despite biographies about the weaknesses of admired Christian notables, character does matter to God. He cannot give Holy Spirit help to hypocrites and frauds or to those who make no effort for God. There must be commitment. If we reach out to please God and walk humbly before him, we can be sure that our *"labor in the Lord is not in vain"* (1 Corinthians 15:58). Where the Holy Spirit provides the tiniest spark, a start can be made.

"Forward"

Bearing such things in mind, what kind of believer does God want? Is there a feature common to all effective workers? For one thing, we know that without faith it is impossible to please him. Grasping the word, too, is the ground of all ministries. It has been said that God creates the right personality for the right hour, but I do not think that is right. Ordinary people have taken up the challenge. They were not made for the time; the times made them. Great characters like Moses, David, Peter, Paul, Luther and Wesley were not born great or unique. Elijah, the most extraordinary figure, was *"a man just like us"* (James 5:17) (Greek *homoiopathes*, "similarly affected"). Men and women who perform lesser exploits than others are not to be judged lesser people. Not everybody can be king or lead the hosts of the Lord. Not everybody could be one of Christ's first disciples, but he said that to give a cup of water to a disciple is an act worthy of a reward (Mark 9:41). "Minor" roles are vital – and so are "nobodies." In Scripture God equipped the least likely characters for his providential purposes.

So, when I think about men and women whom God has used, I know that the finger is usually put on their spirituality, and a close walk with God is certainly not to be ignored. However, one thing that has impressed me about them and that never appears to be mentioned seems to be typical of anyone who ever did anything for God: they were the kind of people that had "get up and go," natural go-getters, perhaps even jumped-up and brash. Moses told the people of Israel to *"stand firm and wait"* but God gave a counter-order, *"Tell the Israelites to go forward"* (Exodus 14:13-15). They may be pushy, forward types, often criticized, but being forward for God is forgivable.

We cannot always help what we are. Some people are shy and quiet, while others are brash and boisterous. We cannot judge their hearts – only God can do that. There is a niche for both in the temple of God. However, it is not always a matter of what we are by birth. Some mistaken Christian teaching on humility makes it a virtue to sit at the back, out of sight. God wants some people at the front, visible. If we treat prominence as a fault, nothing would ever get done. Bible characters who led were humble enough but they knew that someone had to take over and do the essential tasks that no one was doing. God even said that he even looked for someone to stand in the gap and there was nobody (Ezekiel 22:30).

The best known example of "forwardness" is David, tackling the giant when the whole army held back. Great warriors stood in the ranks and David was a stripling. Goliath raged insulted by the chosen champion who seemed unworthy to be his match. David's brothers were all capable warriors. God knew David was a go-getter and so did his brothers. David irritated them with his brash impertinence. They told him to get off the battlefield and go back to looking after his sheep. David stuck to his plan and became the most famous champion in all history, the hero of the day.

God chose David and David's splendid brothers disappeared from the pages of history. They had treated David like Cinderella, the

family "drudge". God chose him, we read, because he was prepared to do everything God wanted him to do (Acts 13:22). People sing, "Sweet will of God, still fold me closer, till I am wholly
lost in thee." That is mere spiritual pose, a monastery achievement,
not good for very much unless it galvanizes people into action for
world salvation.

Profound Assurance in God

Without bold pushiness David would have stayed with his sheep,
but we need to realize that his "go" stemmed from his profound
assurance in God. His "go" and his faith were potent. We are not
told how David acquired his assured faith in God but it was mo-
tivating power feeding his own natural disposition. Without faith
what he did would have been blind presumption. That explains so
much of David's story. David said, *"By my God I can scale a wall"*
(2 Samuel 22:30). That is the man of God every time, all through
history, all around the globe ... "by my God, I can". Some have
"go" but no faith. Whatever our energies, without faith it is impossible to please God. Gumption and trust are the two feet of
those that walk with God.

Another example in Scripture that is not talked about very much
these days is David's friend Jonathan, son of Saul, David's soul
mate. He knew how to rely on God. At that time his father Saul
was king, and his sluggishness had allowed invading Philistine
forces to paralyze Israel. They were squatting right on Israel territory and carrying out raids from their camps to plunder the
harvests.

Jonathan was stationed with a small isolated and inactive detach-
ment of soldiers. They had waited for orders but day after day
Jonathan and his men were kicking their heels, restless and
frustrated. Then, tired of indecision, they decided to take action
on their own. God did not tell them to do anything any more
than God had told David to fight Goliath. Jonathan was clearly

not obedient, for he had no command from King Saul. What he did was an initiative of faith, not an act of obedience. We shall see what happened, but first a word about "obedience."

Obedience is a key Christian word, much emphasized. "Do nothing except in obedience to God," we are told. Because obedience is stressed, believers often do nothing, waiting for a special call that they can obey. The famous hymn says "Trust and obey, for there's no other way to be happy in Jesus," but one needs something to obey. Many wait as obedient servants, and they do just that – wait, but take no action because they have no leading. Half the laziness of the Christian church arises from the desire to be obedient and "not get ahead of God." People do not hear a voice telling them what to do, so they excuse themselves from action. We can all sing, "I'll obey thee, come what may, dear Lord, have thy way," but how do we know we will do that until we know what God wants and nothing is immediately in mind? People will obey if God orders them to do something specific, but they have never known God give them such orders, so they feel quite comfortable staying put. The great saints of God, from Biblical times through to today, put their own finger on the promises of God and go ahead, and that is how the work of God has progressed. The word, not some subjective impulse, is our authority for action.

> Jonathan had no command from King Saul. What he did was an initiative of faith, not an act of obedience.

Let's return to Jonathan. He had no special word or prompting from God. He simply decided to trust God and have a go. On his own initiative he emerged from his hidden camp, drew the attention of the Philistine garrison and challenged them. They rose to the bait. A skirmish took place and God was with Jonathan. That day he routed the Philistine camp and it led to the whole Israel army rising in confidence and gaining a victory over the pillaging Philistines.

That is the sort of thing that God does. He looks out and links arms with anybody who has a go for him, and empowers their daring. Today God calls out across the world, across the churches, and says, "Go!" If anybody hears and goes, he goes with them like his favored friends.

The call of God may not be personal. People talk about the call of Isaiah. He was never "called"; he volunteered. He heard God asking, *"Whom shall I send?"* and decided that it would be him (Isaiah 6:8). He did not feel particularly worthy, describing himself as having "unclean lips" (Isaiah 6:5). Perhaps his language had not been holy. When Isaiah was ready to go, God cleansed his lips and sent him to deliver his word. Isaiah became a prophet who used the most beautiful language of any prophet.

Christ did not give his Great Commission to anybody in particular, nor did he lay down special qualifications. It is a standing invitation to everyone. Godliness and spirituality are wonderful advantages but they are dormant until Christ's word "Go!" is obeyed. Obedience is to the word of God not to feelings and desires.

Some people spend a lifetime cultivating their own soul, seeking some religion to give them peace or religious feelings. Is that all, just one's own soul? Jesus calls us to follow him into the world that has been ravished by the devil to overcome in his name. Others think that their age lets them off; they are too young or too old. Jeremiah thought he was too young, only a child, but God sent him. "Going" launches our spiritual development. It is not an end result. The disciples had the tremendous privilege and advantage of being pupils of the Master of all masters, Jesus. Yet long before he had finished their education he sent them out to do what he was doing. Actually, that was part of their training and always is. We learn by doing. A piano teacher can tell a pupil what to do, but the pupil has to sit at the keyboard doing it, putting in daily practice. That is how he gains the skill.

A key word in the Mark's Gospel is "immediately," or "straightway." It occurs over 40 times, as many occurrences as in the rest of the New Testament. It is thought that Peter was behind Mark's Gospel and Peter was himself an "immediate" man, impetuous. Jesus was the Man for Peter, for he was also a direct action personality. The world itself could not contain the books that could be written about what Jesus did, said John – in only three years! He seemed so unhurried, with time for everybody, but he accomplished more in his brief ministry than any man in a lifetime.

Gripped

Jesus said, *"I have a baptism to undergo, and how distressed I am until it is completed"* (Luke 12:50). The Greek word that has been translated "distressed" means "gripped" or "held by," like the grip of a sickness or like a hold on a prisoner. That baptism was the baptism of judgment for us on the cross. Jesus had come to do God's will and wanted to get on with it, indescribably awful as it was. He constantly spoke of "his hour," the hour in which he would accomplish triumph by crucifixion and glorify God. When the "hour" struck, he went to Jerusalem, the destined place of his battle with evil, and the disciples following behind him were amazed to see the resolute way in which he strode forward. He knew God's schedule and never lagged behind it for a second.

> Christ did not give his Great Commission to anybody in particular, nor did he lay down special qualifications. It is a standing invitation to everyone.

Paul uses the same Greek word *sunecho* in writing to the Corinthians: *"Christ's love compels us"* (2 Corinthians 5:14). It does not mean that he felt rushed, but rather that Christ's love made him unrelenting in his endeavors. He simply got on with the job. If he had waited for propitious times, the world would still be as he had found it. Paul's initiative changed the times. His orders came from the Great Commission.

Christian "going" is not mere dutiful obedience, an obligation, going whether we feel like it or not. "Go" is heart and soul go, motivated by eagerness of spirit. We might get the impression that the first Christians went out immediately ranging the wide world. No mere command could have driven them. They were so full of the good news, full of this Man Christ Jesus, that they could not stay still. In fact, for 20 years Hebrew believers, thousands of them, stayed around Jerusalem and attended the temple, many still as priests. The apostles did not then "go"; perhaps they knew it was best to stay where they were. We cannot judge.

No aimless Drifting

However, some believers did go. Their story starts in Acts 8. The religious leaders had killed Stephen, one of the 7 Hellenists chosen for the catering task in Jerusalem. Having had success in murdering a Christian, the enemies launched further persecution. Many believers fled the city, including those driven out by the work of Saul of Tarsus. They spread the word as far as Phoenicia, Cyprus and Antioch – but to Jews only, probably in the Jewish synagogues. However, Greek believers *"from Cyprus and Cyrene went to Antioch and began to speak to Greeks also, telling them the good news about Jesus"* (Acts 11:20). They took the gospel to their own culture, as did the Jews. The Hellenists (Greek-speaking people) like Philip evangelized the Gentile world.

It is likely that the *"daily distribution of food"* (Acts 6:1) was interrupted, for we never read of it again. The 7 men organizing this work were Greek-speaking because the Greek-speaking widows complained they were not getting their share of the food. One of them was Stephen, who was to be the first Christian martyr. If the daily food distribution was closed down, he did not go home and retire. Without apostolic orders he preached only yards from where the apostles were – so effectively that his opponents *"could not stand up against his wisdom or the Spirit by whom he spoke"* (Acts 6:10).

Then another of the 7 caterers, Philip, left without an appointed task – again, not to go home, sit down and say, "It's no use. They won't let me preach." He went to Samaria. Jesus had told the disciples to go into Judea and Samaria and he had been there himself with tremendous effect (see John 4). Philip preached with signs following, filling the city with joy. Nobody had done anything like that before. In fact, no disciple had ever preached in Samaria before. Here was another David character, brash and bold, but an entrepreneur for God.

> God wants his people to move, and that happens when someone is bold enough and individual enough to step out and go for God; then everyone will follow their lead. That is the kind of leadership needed.

Peter the chief apostle, strongly Jewish, was sent by the Lord to a place that he would never normally have visited, a Gentile home. God got him to go to the house of a Roman officer with the gospel. He told the Christian leaders in Jerusalem, *"The Spirit told me to have no hesitation about going"* (Acts 11:12). What a wonderful way of life! No more aimless drifting. Multitudes live tragic purposeless lives. They live with no "go" and no direction, happy with "bread and circuses" like the Roman plebeians.

Witnesses and evangelists present the true way of life, introducing the Master who will call them, send them, bless them and make life worth something, give them fulfillment. *"Follow me and I will make you ...,"* said Jesus. *"Those who are led by the Spirit of God are sons of God"* (Romans 8:14).

In the church today there is much talk of "leadership." It is not a Bible word and not much of a Bible idea. However, God wants his people to move, and that happens when someone is bold enough and individual enough to step out and go for God; then everyone will follow their lead. That is the kind of leadership needed, not so much appointed leaders to lead organizations but those who will lead others into activity and boldness for God.

Bench hands stay bench hands and fishermen stay fishermen until God puts "go" in their soul. Those who turn to Christ are offered the Great Adventure, a new world order. They receive and are led by the Spirit of God, the source of all creative energy, movement, invention, joy, music, beauty and goodness. God does not lead anyone down a rut. It is his world and we are here to help him, not to live out a dead round of waking, eating and sleeping.

God not only goes with go-getters, but he makes go-getters. Jesus sent them out as a bannered army to conquer the world – with love. As the last verse of Mark's Gospel tells us, the disciples went everywhere and the Lord confirmed his word by the signs that accompanied it.

We are not "Apostles of the Lamb" but Jesus gives us the same aims, leaving no place for hopelessness or depression. In Christ there is no monotony. He never bored anybody. Christ set people going, digging them out of their snug little burrows to rise above their colorless future. He opens the eyes of the blind to the wonder of life walking with him.

If people want to vegetate, they had better steer clear of Jesus. He is the Resurrection and the Life and therefore raises the living dead. Jesus makes apathetic and pathetic folk athletic in the work for him. He heals cripples. Life consists of many things, but Jesus is the lasting joy. The poet Thomas Gray wrote, *"The paths of glory lead but to the grave."* That may be true of human glory, but those who follow Christ's paths are changed from glory to glory and he leads them to heaven. It is heaven because he is there.

Questions

1. From your reading in this chapter, what two things does some-one need who wants to witness to Christ?
2. What is the role of obedience?

CHAPTER 2

Mission Impossible

"Go to Nineveh!"

Jonah 1:2

Nations rarely have ideals other than looking out for their own interests. Israel was the same. As the people of God they should have been different. They had a divine calling but it seemed to have been placed in the file marked "pending."

Israel was created as a people who were to make the name of the Lord known throughout the earth. It would make them a nation of evangelists: the Lord said, *"You are my witnesses"* (Isaiah 44:8). Instead, they became a sorry example of what witnesses could be like. The prophets of Israel declared the Lord was a great God over all the earth, the God of gods. They sang, *"Praise the Lord, all you nations, extol him, all you peoples"* (Psalm 117:1) but nobody did much about it. After 1,000 years they had made the God of Israel known to no other nation. They had fallen down on the job. In Bible language, they were fruitless: *"The vine is dried up and the fig tree is withered"* (Joel 1:12). Jesus cursed a fig tree, the symbol of Israel, because it bore no fruit (Matthew 21:19).

The extent of Israel's ventures in evangelism was when prophets from Judea and Jerusalem exhorted the ten backslidden northern tribes, Samaria, to return to the God of their fathers. Samaria showed them the door back to where they came from. There was little evangelistic activity beyond that.

Absent without Leave

However, one man stepped over Israel's borders, the prophet Jonah. God sent him. He hung back but in the end there was no getting out of it. It certainly needed courage and resolve. Centuries of Israeli custom were against him and Nineveh was not the place for a Sunday School picnic. It was such a savage, fearful and unworthy place that God was anxious about it. He had to get Jonah to go and save them.

Jonah knew God – at least in a way. Nonetheless, the primitive idea that each country had its own deity was still firmly fixed in his mind. When Naaman the leper was healed, he asked if he could take some of the soil of Israel home with him because he believed that the Lord would be with him in the soil. Jonah thought that the Lord was domiciled in Israel and did not overrun other gods' pitches: *"In Judah God is known, his name is great in Israel"* (Psalm 76:1).

Terrified at the thought of confronting Nineveh with their sins, Jonah tried to escape from God by leaving Israel. He took a ship to go as far away as ships went in those days, Tarshish. Perhaps he thought that the further away he went from Israel, the less likely it was that God would be able to reach him.

Tarshish is thought to be the city of Tartessus in south-west Spain, not far from Gibraltar – in the completely opposite direction from Nineveh and on the far side of the Mediterranean. God certainly had Tarshish on his list of places that had *"not heard his fame or seen his glory"* (Isaiah 66:19). That was because Israel had not bothered about people so far away. Thankfully someone took the name of Jesus to Tarshish – but it was not Jonah.

Like Israel in general, Jonah was not happy about an alien nation – Tarshish or Nineveh – seeing God's glory. To Jonah it was a good excuse to board ship. We could call Jonah the prophet who went AWOL – "absent without leave" – but he learned en route that

God was hard to elude. The writer plays with the word "down." Jonah went south instead of north, *"down to Joppa,"* found a ship going to Tarshish, and *"went down into it"* (NKJV). When a storm arose, *"Jonah had gone* [down] *below deck."* Soon after, he was thrown overboard and went down the gullet of the great fish; as he put it, he *"sank down"* to the *"roots of the mountains"* (Jonah 1:1-4,15-17). He could not go down any further. That was the lowest point in his career!

Jonah knew God but what he knew became his problem! Jonah had a high conception of God's character, which was very unusual for his day. The Lord as Jonah knew him was not a God of doom and gloom. Yet that same God had sent him to proclaim gloom and doom to Nineveh! Jonah frankly did not believe that God could ever bring himself to fulfill such negative prophesies. He said, *"That is why I was so quick to flee to Tarshish. I knew that you are a gracious and compassionate God"* (Jonah 4:2).

I must point out that Jonah was the first international preacher. His audience was people notorious for their hideous cruelties, merciless and wicked. God had to intervene, as with the genetically corrupt people of the antediluvian world as well as Sodom and Gomorrah. Yet he sent Jonah to Nineveh out of divine concern for the people's fate – just as he had sent Abraham to Sodom and Noah to the pre-flood world, to give them a last chance. That is also why he sent us Christ. He is our last chance.

Jonah was confused. He knew God, but he had also inherited some strange ideas. God told him to go to Nineveh but he *"ran away from the Lord and headed for Tarshish"* (Jonah 1:3). Did he presume that by leaving Israel's territory he would leave God behind? Desperation taught him a different lesson. In his terror at having been swallowed by a monster fish, he found himself hoping that God was within earshot after all, although a sea monster's stomach was hardly holy ground. He also knew that a fish has two exits and prayed to find the right one.

Jonah's experience was pretty awful but an important truth emerged from it. At first he thought that God had been left behind, but Jonah became a prime Bible example of the discovery that God is as much in one place as another, even down at the bottom of the mountains or on the far sides of the sea. Although he felt as if he had been "banished" from God's sight, he still thought prayer was worth a try. He said, *"In my distress I called to the Lord and he answered me"* (Jonah 2:1). Necessity helped him to discover that God hears prayer from anywhere, even inside a sea monster. From where would he not hear prayer? What place is not sacred? Jerusalem and the temple have no monopoly on God – nor has any other city. *"Where can I go from your Spirit? Where can I flee from your presence?"* (Psalm 139:7).

No haphazard God

Whereas Jonah ran away from the place where he thought God was, some run away from where they think God is **not**. Many believers think they can find God more somewhere else. If they do not find God's "blessing" or "power" in one place, they go to where there is "revival" – as if God exists more in some places than others. Does God distribute himself in patches? Does he move around erratically and come down like showers on the weather chart? He is not a haphazard God. If we have to travel here and there to experience God, then we have failed to learn something vital. Paul the apostle would not approve of a spiritual nomadic experience. He said, *"Do not say in your heart, 'Who will bring Christ down?' or 'Who will bring Christ up from the dead?' The word is near you; it is in your mouth and in your heart"* (Romans 10:6-8). There is no need to travel to find God at his best. He is always at his best, everywhere. He does not have off days. Those who seek will find but do not need an airline to help them to track God down.

Jonah's preaching was a success. The king ordered repentance in sackcloth and with fasting. Maybe Jonah was pleased but, then again, maybe he wasn't. He had proclaimed judgment on Nineveh, so what would God do now? If Jonah knew God, there would be no judgment, only mercy. His prophetic pride would be hurt. This was just what he feared – that God was too merciful to do what he sent Jonah to say he would do.

That is still our evangelistic paradox. We are not sent to proclaim a message of hell. Our message is of Christ's redeeming and saving love. However, it makes no sense if there is no hell, no doom for the sinful, for without it what are people to be saved from? If Jesus saves, it must be because people need to be saved.

Divine Light of Compassion

What Jonah knew about God was shared by few other people in those days. He expressed it in a statement about God which is a classic: *"I knew that you are a gracious and compassionate God, slow to anger and abounding in love, a God who relents from sending calamity"* (Jonah 4:2). This was the revelation that God had previously given to Moses (Exodus 34:6). It also inspired the prophet Micah. He wrote, *"Who is a God like you, who pardons sin and forgives transgression. You do not stay angry for ever but delight to show mercy"* (Micah 7:18).

There are echoes of this in the words of other prophets. In one of the most moving passages in the Bible, for example, God speaks through the prophet Hosea, pleading, *"How can I give you up, Ephraim? How can I hand you over, Israel? How can I treat you like Admah? How can I make you like Zeboim? My heart is changed within me, all my compassion is aroused"* (Hosea 11:8). This is the heart cry of God. His patient concern is inexhaustible.

The divine light of compassion has always shone across the wasteland of dark years. Compassion, mercy, forgiveness – a rolling tide of kindness, an inner driving force for men like Moses, Micah, Hosea and then the apostles. *"Christ's love compels us,"* said Paul (2 Corinthians 5:14).

What a revelation! If we are not moved by it, the very core of the word, how can we move others? Jonah's classic statement should be our greatest motivation, even if it was not his. The world is wicked and we might look around scornfully, even thinking, like Jonah, that they deserve hell. We need to remember that we are part of that wicked world except for God's amazing grace. If we look at the world, the world looks at us. If we go public with the gospel, is the kindness of God in our eyes?

After Nineveh repented, Jonah sat outside the city waiting to see if God would still destroy it after all (Jonah 4:5). He felt a fool, preaching judgment when he felt sure none would come if God could avoid it. God had let him down by being so merciful.

Jonah had one concern – himself. The fate of the entire population of the world's greatest city was less important to him than his own reputation as a prophet. He had not preached out of anxiety for the multitudes of men, women and children. He did it because he dared not disobey God again. The last time he was swallowed by some engulfing horror from the deep. What would happen the next time he disobeyed?

Jonah's interest was himself, number one and all figures to ten. He was a prophet of God yet aboard ship nobody knew it. He did not even pray during the storm, which shocked the pagan crew. They woke him up and told him to cry out to his God. Chapter 2 describes him praying *"from inside the fish"* – not about God saving the sinners in Nineveh but about himself. He used "I, me, my" over and over again.

Jonah, the reluctant evangelist, was no match for the Lord, the determined Savior! This discredited man had amazing success because God needed his input for his overflowing compassion to take effect. The Lord has invested everything in the work of salvation: *"God did not spare his own Son but gave him up for us all"* (Romans 8:32). The only way God could give in a way that it was costly to him was through the indescribable gift of his Son. God's view of the world is like his view of the pre-flood world, of Sodom and Gomorrah and of Nineveh: it desperately needs to be saved from the impending judgment.

So what about reluctant evangelists? Let's be honest, are we all so keen to proclaim the truth? Are our prayers all "I" – "me" – "my"? Jesus said, *"Go into all the world and preach the good news to all creation"* (Mark 16:15). Are these just nice words for our morning devotions? If we hear and do nothing then how can his words help us? If we do take action, the approval of God is guaranteed. We can move along with him in his great purpose as he does his saving work. But what if we don't?

Questions

1. Why did Jonah think he could run away from God?
2. Why did he run away?
3. In terms of our own lives, how can we "run away"?

For the Lord your God
will be with you wherever you go.
Do not be terrified;
do not be discouraged!

Joshua 1:9

CHAPTER 3

Apostolic Cruise

"The Spirit of Jesus would not allow them."

Acts 16:7

Paul set out for Mysia and Bithynia to carry out Christ's Great Commission. Then the Spirit stopped him! That is amazing. The initial progress of the gospel depended on Paul and his helpers, but the Holy Spirit stopped them in their tracks!

Redundant?

How did they feel? Redundant? God had left Paul and his team with nothing to do! There they were, on board of a ship, forced into inactivity, with no signs of what God might want. We know God was with them … although they were away from the action.

That is a situation worth noting. The Lord stood by them when they were not actively engaged in his work – just as much as when they were. We need to remember that everything we do should be regarded as "for the Lord." Paul traveled where and when he wanted. He has set off for Mysia and Bithynia as he thought fit, with no specific word from God, but God worked with him everywhere. Only on rare occasions did he have a specific sign from God to go, stay, or leave.

God leaves us to plan but never leaves us. He can – and sometimes will – step in with a specific revelation of his purpose but he is with us, watching over us, at all times. The gospel is far too important – as are our own personal lives, too – for God to leave us totally without his oversight. Mark 16:20 tells us that the first evangelists went when and where they thought fit, but the Lord always went with them. God is always two steps ahead.

Acts 16:7 says that *"the Spirit of Jesus would not allow them"* to enter Bithynia – negative guidance. In our first years in Africa, we established a new missionary field which expanded and out-stripped normal missionary station activity, becoming a responsi-bility that was too big for the mission's board mandate. I eventu-ally had to leave the mission but the Lord gave me no notion of what he wanted next.

We packed our possessions and moved out, ready to start all over again. We had no sign of what or how. I was frustrated, too dis-tressed even to unpack, sitting beside the road on a crate of our possessions with my head in my hands. I felt so alone and full of questions. Day after day, week after week, heaven remained silent; it was like living Psalm 74:9: *"We are given no miraculous signs; no prophets are left."*

I knew the book of Acts and could have drawn hope from Chapter 16 if we had realized what was going on. That verse fitted my situation: *"The Spirit of Jesus would not allow them."* Paul and his friends were full of zeal to go into all the world in obedience to Christ's final words on earth. They planned to push across north Asia Minor (now Turkey), to evangelize Mysia, Bithynia and the region of Asia. Yet the Spirit forbade it!

Nor did the Spirit give them an alternative route. Their big plans collapsed. They could only stay where they were, on board ship in the Aegean Sea. We are not told whether they worried about that. They could do nothing except sail on. God had organized it and there was no option. I identified with those early pioneers, doing nothing and going nowhere.

Why should God want it that way? Well, why shouldn't he? Is God so desperate for help that he must keep everybody at it all the time? In Acts we find evidence to the contrary – God side-lined even Paul on that ship. As for me, was I the only one around? Couldn't he afford to lose a day of my help?

I did not understand then but I see now why he had me at home doing nothing. That was where he wanted me; I was where he had planted me. Paul had been *"kept by the Holy Spirit from preaching the word in the province of Asia"* (Acts 16:6) and Paul lived under guard for a couple of years in Caesarea, where he seems to have done nothing, not even writing a letter.

> The gospel is far too important – as are our own personal lives, too – for God to leave us totally without his oversight.

We know Paul was destined to make a bigger impact on the world. I could take heart; if such a giant, why not others – me, for example? He was now giving me a breathing space. Actually, I was standing on the threshold of my life's work of unprecedented opportunities and responsibilities.

Paul eventually left ship at Troas, but that was not what God had in mind for them. The apostolic team had no urge to preach there. Why would soon be apparent. Across the Aegean Sea, 200 miles from the eastern Troas, lay Thrace (Greece) and Macedonia, gateways to the whole continent of Europe.

Putting Things together

The future, progress and civilization were westward, not eastward, where Paul's plans lay. One night at Troas Paul had a vision. He saw a man saying, *"Come over to Macedonia and help us"* (Acts 16:9). This small apostolic group had no idea of their own immense importance. The future of Europe and the world lay in their hands. Paul did not know it but God did, and in that historic hour the seed of world change germinated.

Now, Paul did not jump up at once saying, "The Lord told me!" If we say "the Lord told me," it had better be the Lord and not spiritual conceit. Paul and his colleagues *"concluded"* (Greek *sumbibazo*

– put things together) that Lord wanted them to switch from the east and move westward into Macedonia – a major change of plan. Paul saw it as an opportunity – not a divine command; Paul's God was not a "boss-God" but a fellow-worker. God was moving and Paul moved with him.

Obviously, they had sailed for Mysia and Bithynia with no directive from God, but that was not a mistake or failure. If God did not speak then, he had nothing to say to them at that time, that is all. God is not a machine to set in motion, talking on demand. Christ's Great Commission, to preach to all creation everywhere, gave them carte blanche. Paul pioneered with his own road map of circumstances and inclinations, ready for God to re-route him if necessary. He had always worked like that, and God re-routed him on only half a dozen or so occasions.

Paul told the Thessalonians that he had wanted to visit them but that *"Satan stopped"* him (1 Thessalonians 2:18). He knew when it was Satan and when it was God. In either case the gospel went forward. On another occasion, he was planning to visit the Corinthians but stayed on at Ephesus because he said, *"a great door for effective work has opened to me"* (1 Corinthians 16:9). Again, he did not say, "The Lord told me to stay." Common sense is God-given, for us to use, and God does not usually override it.

Paul wrote to Rome, *"I do not want you to be unaware, brothers, that I planned many times to come to you, but have been prevented from doing so until now. I pray that now at last by God's will the way may be opened for me to come to you"* (Romans 1:13,10). Notice that he wrote *"I planned"* and then speaks of *"God's will."* He had no reason to think that his plan was other than God's will. Then towards the end of his letter he wrote again about the possibility of visiting them on his way to Spain and asked for their prayers. He made plans but accepted circumstances, knowing the Lord could not be frustrated.

Paul and his colleagues were never anxious. They assumed that the Lord was in control. I know many people who sincerely seek and wait each day for God's instructions, but guidance does not depend on our seeking it; if we seek to obey, God guides. Guidance is not a favor bestowed on us for the asking. It is too important for that. If we are willing, he keeps us on track. Some even worry that God may have spoken when they happened not to be listening, but if God had something to say, he would not whisper; he would make sure we heard. A father does not whisper his wishes to his son, nor does our heavenly Father.

Paul had warnings from prophets and words from the Lord but knew God had plans for him and never deviated from his course, even when it was heart-breaking. *"None of these things move me,"* he said (Acts 20:24 KJV). God does not change his mind every half-day. Along the way, we may pass through circumstances which give us hope and suggest future vistas or others which give us little hope, with seemingly no meaning. Nevertheless, his great purposes move on like the earth in its course.

Being on the Way

There are plenty of maxims bandied about as if they were Scripture but they are just popular philosophy, e.g. "Don't move till God tells you"; "Always wait for God." They sound so humble and spiritual but we search for them in the Bible in vain. Moses himself told the tribes of Israel, *"Do not be afraid. Stand firm and you will see the deliverance the Lord will bring you today"* (Exodus 14:13). God told Moses to stop praying and get off the ground. He gave a counter-command: *"Tell the Israelites to move on"* (Exodus 14:15).

The apostles also "moved on"; they did not fast and pray for a month to find out what they were supposed to do. They preached everywhere and their cue was the word of Eliezer, Abraham's chief servant: *"As for me, being on the way, the Lord led me"* (Genesis 24:27). Nowhere does the word tell us to do nothing until we hear God's instructions; it tells us to put everything into whatever our hand finds to do. Joshua was ready to invade the Promised Land, so God told him to go ahead *"for the Lord your God will be with you wherever you go. Do not be terrified; do not be discouraged!"* (Joshua 1:9). All the way God respected Joshua's decisive leadership and went along with him. The promise of God is that *"Whatever he does prospers"* – a promise for those whose roots go down into the word, like into fertile soil (Psalm 1:3). *"Do not let this Book of the Law depart from your mouth; be careful to do everything written in it. Then you will be prosperous and successful"* (Joshua 1:8).

The Lord directs those who are on the way. It is impossible to steer a bicycle until it is moving. A steering wheel is useless in a car with a flat battery. God does not want servants like puppets, moving only when he pulls the strings, dancing only to his tune. Scripture contains no such suggestion.

Horses never know when or where to go until they feel the bit and bridle, but Psalm 32:9 says we should not be like that, expecting God to tell us when to put a foot forward. We are not horses. Horses have no wisdom. We have, and we are told to *"walk in wisdom,"* not in blind obedience (Colossians 4:5 NKJV). Again and again we are assured that the Lord will direct our steps and that we will hear his voice saying, *"This is the way, walk in it"* (Isaiah 30:21). In fact, the major Bible theme of the Great Shepherd says the same thing, Jesus shepherds us – which is a lot more than leading.

Some believe that God will guide only if they pray long and hard about it and listen very closely. That is a strange picture of God. Does he really need persuading to tell us what he wants, responding only in a quiet murmur?

It is presumption to maintain that God must always have new instructions for us. God may be happy for you to stay where you are.

Guidance is God's business and it is not our business to tell him to guide. He always guides if we are prepared to be guided. *"Those who are led by the Spirit of God are sons of God"* (Romans 8:14). If we are not being led, are we his sons?

To go on the Lord's business, careless about his presence spells failure. The Holy Spirit is the *pneuma* of God. We use the word *pneuma* for many modern appliances that use air, such as automobile tires. If we take that practical example, without *pneuma* – air – a pneumatic tire is flat. Without faith in God's presence at all times, life is like driving on flat tires or setting sail without winds. Without God's Spirit to keep us moving, we get nowhere.

Paul could never have visualized the later outcome of his change of plans. For 1,400 years Europe's culture has been shaped by the message of that man, just a harried, knocked-about little evangelist whom some people mocked. None of us can know what future depends on us, on our work, loyalty, courage, friendships, and marriage. To live without God is not only a waste of life but leaves no mark on life whatever, only footprints in the sand. God has no trivial pursuits, no casual aims. Our lives are best led by him. We can all be involved in the will of God and its vast and eternal outcome, or we can be left out as of no consequence. *"It is not for man to direct his own steps"* (Jeremiah 10:23).

Questions

1. How do we react to situations in which nothing seems to move?
2. What do we understand about God's guidance?

This is love:
not that we loved God,
but that he loved us and sent his Son
as an atoning sacrifice for our sins.

1 John 4:10

CHAPTER 4

When Romans gave in

"The message of the cross"
1 Corinthians 1:18

The sign of the cross is the most powerful symbol in the world. The death of Christ is the pivot of time, the Rock that never rocks, standing in the sea of history, with the waves beating against it but never moving it. No technology can take its place. It is our sole but abiding hope.

A cynical world asks, "What has God done for me?" The short answer is, what has he not done for you? He had done everything, given you existence and now offers you eternal redemption. He is the creator and redeemer.

Christ died for us. That event was a cosmic explosion of love and goodness, shattering the rock-solid walls and iron gates of every bondage that ever tyrannized mankind to open up the eternal purposes of God.

A check for a billion dollars would seem nothing crammed into a pocket, but it opens vast possibilities to the payee. That Friday deed in the darkness changes everything. Jesus the Carpenter turned the wood of his cross into the door of heaven.

The average Christian enjoys a quality of life that no other religion offers even to its most ardent seekers. Only Jesus saves because only Jesus died to be able to offer what he offers. Nobody else stands where he stands.

If we mean business in evangelism, we need to look at the first gospel message ever preached. Delivered by the apostle Peter, it was based on the crucifixion and resurrection of Jesus. There is no Christianity without that. If Christ's death and resurrection are problems to anyone, it is because they have not experienced the power of either of them. Peter proclaimed the saving power of the crucified Jesus and that alone is the key to the kingdom. Those who do not preach it shut the gates of the kingdom in the face of life's pilgrims.

> The sign of the cross is the most powerful symbol in the world. The death of Christ is the pivot of time, the Rock that never rocks, standing in the sea of history, with the waves beating against it but never moving it.

The most wonderful "mystery" is that of the redeeming death of Christ. We shall never know its depths because what happened lay mainly in the heart of Jesus and the Father. The cross impacts people's minds in many ways. Some think of Jesus as a martyr – a reject. Others see the agony of Christ as a picture of the world's agony. He was certainly one with it all. He achieved solidarity with us and bound God into our world and its woes. We need not ask, "Where is God?" We look at the cross and see him there, sharing the heartbreak, shame and pain. But what did it actually do? Apart from our reactions, did it achieve anything?

Christianity in Great Britain has been attributed to the story of King Edwin, who was baptized in AD 627. An assassin raised his sword to kill him but one of the attendants stepped between the two men and took the fatal blow, dying for the king. It helped the king and others to understand the cross, where Jesus had stepped in and taken the fatal thrust of the sword of divine justice for us. The king was converted to Christianity.

Salvation through the blood of Jesus has sometimes been put so crudely that it has turned many away. Scripture is exact and our evangelism should keep to sounding Biblical teaching.

General Guide

We are told of Christ's executioners: *"Sitting down, they kept watch over him there"* (Matthew 27:36); they were on guard duty in case Christ's followers should attempt to take him down from the cross. The horrific spectacle of a young man covered in blood, savaged and mangled, was to them a matter of mockery. Yet, in their own lifetime their helpless victim would be the most loved of all men and for 2,000 years revered as God, worshipped by ten times more than the population of the whole Roman Empire.

People speak of the world's ten greatest battles but not one of them has had such absolute effects as Christ's battle with death. His death-wrack, the cross, is engraved on mankind's memory, a symbol of both absolute wickedness and absolute love.

That is the mystery of the cross. Seven weeks after the mob howled for his blood, Peter publicly accused them: *"You, with the help of wicked men, put him to death by nailing him to the cross. Let all Israel be assured of this: God has made this Jesus, whom you crucified, both Lord and Christ"* (Acts 2:23,36). The effect was astonishing and could never have been anticipated. The preaching of the cross brought 3,000 people to repentance. The first names were written in the Lamb's book of life.

Christ crucified has been the core of the Christian gospel ever since. No gospel could be stranger. Religions point to their great founders but to make a gospel, a good news message, out of a man's execution, and especially to address the authorities as responsible for it, seemed futile madness. Yet Paul said, *"I am eager to preach the gospel to you who are at Rome. I am not ashamed of the gospel"* (Romans 1:15). To Roman citizens in Corinth he declared, *"I resolved to know nothing while I was with you except Jesus Christ and him crucified"* (1 Corinthians 2:2). Paul knew such a message would be a *"stumbling block"* to Jews and *"foolishness"* to everybody else (1 Corinthians 1:23) but he preached it just the same. The world heard and changed. That message looked decidedly unlikely to transform a degraded age – but it did.

The executioners' hands were covered with the blood of Jesus, but he prayed *"Father forgive them!"*, and that same blood cleansed them. That message remains the message. Christ crucified has no competitors. What is the secret of the cross? What is it about it that makes it what it is? Let's spend a brief minute or two thinking about it.

The Secret of the Cross

First, the event itself is deeply moving. He, the only perfectly good person, bore the unbearable for love's sake. It is a spectacle that still clutches at the heart. We sing, "When I survey the wondrous cross on which the Prince of glory died, my richest gain I count but loss, and pour contempt on all my pride."

Surely nothing has ever brought emotions to the surface like the death of Christ. However, to move people by the spectacle, is that all the cross does? Would that emotion change a drug addict or stop a murderer? Weeping at the sight, would it bring a conviction or forgiveness?

As the hymn says, the sight of the cross may humble our pride and demand our life for something (for what?), but did Jesus die just to humble us? If he died as an example, an example of what? Just dying is no example. There had to be a purpose.

Scripture describes Christ's sufferings: *"I offered my back to those who beat me, my cheeks to those who pulled out my beard; I did not hide my face from mocking and spitting"* (Isaiah 50:6). The Roman squad watched the horrible scene but it did not convert them.

Paul complained to the Galatians, *"Christ was clearly portrayed as crucified"* but the picture had not saved them (Galatians 3:1). Their faith was missing and they had drifted off into legalism.

Paul did not dramatize the cross to move his hearers, hoping by his eloquence to make the event stark and real and to turn pagan sinners into Christian saints. How could it? There has to be a great power involved. Paul preached what the death of Christ was about, that he died redemptively, bearing away our sins. It made Paul what he was: *"I live by faith in the Son of God, who loved me and gave himself for me"* (Galatians 2:20). The gospel is not good news that Christ died, but that he died for us, died our death, blocked the judgment of God against us and released us from condemnation.

The power of the cross was far more than its emotional effect. Something went on at the cross that nothing else could achieve. Let's follow a strand or two of this great Bible truth.

> Christ's death-wrack, the cross, is engraved on mankind's memory, a symbol of both absolute wickedness and absolute love.

A special episode occurs when Jesus told his disciples, *"The Son of Man must suffer many things and he must be killed and on the third day be raised to life"* (Luke 9:22). Note that little word *"must."* Why did he have to go through those things? He took three disciples to a mountain where a wonderful thing happened. Jesus became gloriously transfigured and two characters from the past re-appeared, Moses and Elijah.

The disciples were overwhelmed by what they saw and heard the heavenly beings talking to Jesus about dying and how great an event that death would be. It was obviously the talk of heaven. We read, *"They spoke about his departure, which he was about to bring to fulfillment at Jerusalem"* (Luke 9:31). The Greek word translated "departure" is our word "exodus" (*exodos*), which makes us think of Israel's deliverance from Egypt, a mighty manifestation of divine power. Death is spoken about as an exodus only twice in Scripture, the second time being when Peter (who had been with Jesus on the mountain) spoke of his own death. He had learned there that death really is a triumphant event.

When Jesus died, he shouted with a loud voice. No dying man other than Jesus has ever done that. In that moment he surrendered his life to God, crying, *"It is finished!"* (Greek: *tetelestai*, from *teleo*). The Roman centurion heard that. He had seen men die but never so triumphantly and he said, *"Surely this was a righteous man. Surely he was the Son of God"* (Luke 23:47, Matthew 27:54).

The Greek word *tetelestai* means more than the word "finished"; it means "accomplished," "concluded." A related Greek word is used in John 17:4; Jesus prayed, *"I have brought you glory on earth by completing* [Greek: *teleioósas*] *the work you gave me to do."* The word occurs again in John 13:1 (NKJV): *"Having loved his own who were in the world he loved them to the end"* (Greek: *eis telos*).

Describing Christ's sufferings many centuries before they occurred, Isaiah said, *"He was led like a lamb to the slaughter and as a sheep before her shearers is silent, so he did not open his mouth"* (Isaiah 53:7). He submitted to his enemies but he did not have to; he could have slain them with a word. It looks as if Jesus died as a helpless victim but in that lay his greatness and love. He went to the cross for us, an achievement against all odds, God in Christ against evil.

On the cross Christ did more than touch our feelings, he fulfilled a purpose that he had chosen and that he had talked about all the way through his ministry. He often spoke about his forthcoming death. *"Now is my heart troubled, and what shall I say? Father, save me from this hour? No, it was for this very reason came I to this hour"* (John 12:27).

"This hour" – there had been great hours when Jesus healed the sick, raised the dead, and taught the multitudes. But during those hours he spoke of "the hour" when his life's objective would be realized, the consummation of all that he lived for. That hour was his last hour when he died an atoning death.

Death was his aim. He came to confront that enemy. He came to destroy the works of the devil. We avoid death, taking proper care against accidents, diseases and other dangers. Death pursues us; as Scripture says, *"We who are alive are always being given over to death"* (2 Corinthians 4:11). Jesus was not pursued by death; he pursued and challenged death. He forced the king of terrors to keep an appointment with him, a duel. He cornered the enemy, grappled with the awful reality and *"tasted death for everyone"* (Hebrew 2:9). The picture is of Christ in the role of a champion warrior, entering into the domain of death and overcoming it, causing the "death of death," as the hymn says.

The first reference to the battle on the cross is Genesis 3:15: the seed of the woman would crush the head of the serpent but his own heel would be bruised. Jesus also spoke of being "distressed" until it was done (Luke 12:50). The word means pressed, constrained, gripped with an intention. He constantly anticipated his encounter with death, the great enemy.

In the Garden of Gethsemane and at Calvary he grasped the serpent of death, strangled the life out of it and returned from the fight three days later bearing the scars of battle but crowned with victory for us all. *"Our Savior, Jesus Christ, has destroyed death and has brought life and immortality to light"* (2 Timothy 1:10). *"He too shared in their humanity so that by his death he might destroy him who holds the power of death — that is, the devil"* (Hebrew 2:14). The Greek word *katargeo*, which is translated "destroy," means to be emptied of strength, to be made inactive, useless. The day of victory has come about as a result of Christ's triumph, when *"death has been swallowed up in victory"* (1 Corinthians 15:54).

> The gospel is not good news that Christ died, but that he died for us, died our death, blocked the judgment of God against us and released us from condemnation.

The serpent of death lost its sting, but what was its sting? *"Where, O death, is your sting? The sting of death is sin"* (1 Corinthians 15:55-56). The real horror of death is to die in our sins, passing into the beyond laden with guilt. We have little idea what that means, but it was so horrendous Christ died to save us from it and make an end of it. He died not only to destroy death but to destroy our sins. On the cross Christ milked the serpent fangs of its poison and we can cry out, *"Where, O death, is your victory? Where, O death, is your sting?"*

What is sin? It is the effect on God of human rebellion. Wickedness touches God. He senses all injustice, merciless cruelty, hatred, wrong and evil. He senses it because he loves us all. His reaction is not that of an offended dignity but of a Father. *"Against you, you only, have I sinned,"* said David (Psalm 51:4). As an absolute monarch, David was above the law but he was not above God. God is not indifferent to what is going on. He is wounded, stabbed by human willfulness as hostility against his very heart and infinitely holy being. The polluted streams of sinfulness drain into the pained heart of God.

When Christ went to the cross as the Son of God, he had always born our sins, but as the Son of Man he bore our sins away. He knew the dreadful load and its physical horrors and spiritual blackness and became sin for us, endured our judgment hell, standing between us and the fate we deserved. Jesus brought us eternal forgiveness. God did not blame him or make him guilty, but he bore our judgment for us as our great Second Adam, our representative.

The gospel truth is that evil is not only forgiven but mastered, overcome. Jesus overcame the worst the devil could do. This was the promise: *"I will forgive their wickedness and will remember their sins no more"* (Jeremiah 31:34). Nothing of it remains in his mind or heart to haunt or condemn us.

Seeing Christ's agony on the cruel cross affects us. We weep. Yet he did not die to make us weep, an empty gesture, but offered himself to God on the cross to effect eternal salvation. He wrought a change in the divine order, rendering sin and death impotent. *"God was in Christ reconciling the world to himself, not imputing their trespasses to them"* (2 Corinthians 5:19).

If we preach any other gospel, it is not the gospel of Christ. To omit the horrors of the cross, to soft-pedal those events is to betray the world, for it would die without it. No other message from all the religions or all the books can truly ease our conscience and bring us the hope of God.

Hanging on the cross, Christ displayed the full extent of his love. How? If a man told his wife, "I love you and I'll prove it by shooting myself," that man would be insane. How could suicide prove a man loved his wife? It did nothing for her. However, if he was shot trying to protect her, losing his life to save her, that would be love. That is how Christ died for us, not for the sake of dying, but to die for us and save us. Our sins would destroy us but *"he himself bore our sins in his own body on the tree"* (1 Peter 2:24) – or, as another Bible translation puts it, *"he carried away our sins in his own body on the cross"* (NLT).

> Christ died for us, not for the sake of dying, but to die for us and save us. Our sins would destroy us but *"he himself bore our sins in his own body on the tree"*.

That gives us some idea of the curse that sin is; God himself had to intervene and bear the whole brunt of evil himself. God keeps the whole order of nature together. It shows his love for his creatures, but he never mentioned that. One thing he did say: *"God so loved the world that he gave his one and only Son"* (John 3:16). God never did anything greater than give his Son. He had nothing greater to give or do. It was the only true sacrifice possible to God. Creating more worlds was nothing in comparison. Giving every one of us the wealth of a whole planet would cost him nothing but in giving his Son, he gave everything he had.

A billionaire might show some love by buying his son a Rolls Royce but, better than that, he can give him his time attention and affection. God did not just give us gifts; he gave himself: *"This is love: not that we loved God, but that he loved us and sent his Son as an atoning sacrifice for our sins"* (1 John 4:10).

It is a staggering fact, but it took all God had to save us! It took Jesus to come, weep, and pray for us in the garden, to be arrested and to submit to the most unendurable treatment, and to experience the sword of divine judgment piercing his body. That is what he did and it tells us what our plight was. Only God could save us.

That is why we preach Christ crucified. It is the promise of salvation guaranteed by this tremendous act of God in Christ, no cheap forgiveness at the snap of a finger. God had to go to such lengths for people, we had better tell them about it.

Questions

1. Why is an emotional view of the cross inadequate?
2. In what two ways did God in Christ bear our sins?

CHAPTER 5

Agency of Revolution

"As servants of God, we commend ourselves in every way."

2 Corinthians 6:4

The greatest and most moving Scripture chapter about ministry is probably 2 Corinthians 6. Paul wrote this letter to the Corinthians after hearing disturbing news and he feared damage to the church. He wrote to them *"so that our ministry will not be discredited"* (v 3).

Countering lofty Claims

Paul appealed to the Corinthians, describing his own attitude and that of his team. At all costs, their aim was to *"commend ourselves in every way as servants of God"*. (v 4). I echo that wish here, and in this chapter I want to take up things that Paul wrote to the Corinthians about gospel witness needing to be through life as well as lip.

Believers in Corinth were being exploited by men asserting themselves as true apostles. They claimed that Paul lacked the marks of true apostleship. Paul actually worked with his hands and was humble and patient, whereas they considered that people of real caliber were strong and proud and that work was for slaves. That was the spirit of all noble Romans. In Roman society, class colored attitudes. The rich and famous were considered good. Paul did not fit the mould.

Certain characters came to Corinth and were welcomed as men of status – in true Roman style. The believers fell prey to their lordly airs as super-apostles. Paul was amazed: *"You even put up with anyone who enslaves you or exploits you or takes advantage of you or pushes himself forward or slaps you in the face"* (2 Corinthians 11:20). It was an astounding situation. Something of the arrogance of these new super-apostles rubbed off on the Corinthian believers, as we discern from Paul's remarks about their claims of knowledge and spiritual gifts.

Paul had to assert his apostolic authority in Christ, who he was and what he had done. He called it "foolish boasting" but it was necessary to challenge the jumped-up false apostles. He contrasted their lordly and acquisitive life style with the Christian lifestyle of those who follow Jesus, mentioning his own sacrifices and treatment at the hands of his opponents. He had been battered and despised, suffering shame, deprivation and imprisonment – hardly things to boast about. It pointed to a major difference between him and the false apostles' lofty claims. He "boasted" of his labors and even of his weakness, saying that when he was weak, then he was strong (2 Corinthians 12:10).

"Five times I received from the Jews forty lashes minus one. Three times I was beaten with rods, once I was stoned, three times I was shipwrecked, I spent a night and day in the open sea, I have been constantly on the move. I have been in danger from rivers, in danger from bandits, in danger from my own countrymen, in danger from Gentiles; in danger in the city, in danger in the country, and in danger from false brothers. I have labored and toiled and have often gone without sleep; I have often known hunger and thirst and have often gone without food; I have been cold and naked." (2 Corinthians 11:24-27)

A man like that does not sound very important. If he were a somebody, would the world be contemptuous of him, beating him? Would he need to work at a rough and humble job to earn a living? A "somebody" would never have been in such straits in Roman times. He had none of the qualities Romans admired – money, power, success. Paul practiced only weaknesses, poverty, humility, gentleness, forgiveness, and patience. He was a preacher, but even in that he confessed to preaching in fear and trembling and had no persuasive tongue.

The real Thing

This was wisdom to Paul. He wanted the power of God to be evident. If people turned to Christ because of Paul's force of character and argumentative skill, how could the power of God be seen? That is something for us to think about in our own times.

Paul wanted the real thing – Christ – to be all in all. He said that followers of Christ need to *"clothe themselves with Christ,"* take off the old proud nature, and walk humbly (Romans 13:14, Colossians 3:12). I once asked a lady what she did for Jesus and her reply was "I do toilet duty for the children in Sunday school." Somebody had to do that job and she chose it, just like somebody had to wash the feet of Christ's disciples after they had walked through the dirty streets, and Jesus chose to do it.

Paul had been a real personality in the land before his conversion. He had changed his name from the great Saul to the diminutive Paul, and lived a life of selfless dedication. It qualified him now to exhort the Corinthians to new attitudes. He wrote the greatest exhortation to love ever penned – 1 Corinthians 13. *"We make ourselves a model for you to follow"* (2 Thessalonians 3:9).

Proud characters in Corinth arrogated to themselves the role of apostles and collected their followers. Let us hope they have no counterparts in our churches today. Jude delivered a strong warning about *"flattering others for their own advantage"* (v 16). Many a church has been disrupted and leaders discouraged when someone has come in, flattering and charming people in order to siphon off their own following. To lead, gather, and inspire backers for the work of God is one thing, but to advance one's own interests for personal advantage, for one's ego, is another – like what the super-apostles were doing in Corinth.

Paul now draws the road map not only for evangelists, but for all Christian witnesses. *"As God's fellow-workers we urge you not to receive God's grace in vain"* (2 Corinthians 6:1). He wrote that to believers, not the unconverted: "Don't receive God's grace pointlessly!" Grace is accompanied by obligations. Paul quoted Isaiah, *"In the time of my favor I heard you, and in the day of salvation I helped you"* and added, *"I tell you, now is the time of God's favor, now is the day of salvation"* (2 Corinthians 6:2).

Paul was writing to people who had experienced salvation, but it looked as if it could all amount to nothing and that they would fail in witness and bring the ministry into disrepute. Paul and Timothy were *"God's fellow-workers,"* but what were the Corinthians doing? It was a matter for urgent attention. "Now is the day of salvation" – not tomorrow. In Corinth, witness was not only hard but dangerous. Would it be easier later on? Light is needed when the darkness is deepest. Psalm 126:6 speaks of sowing in tears and in all weathers: *"He who goes out weeping, carrying seed to sow, will return with songs of joy, carrying sheaves with him."* Cold winds brought tears to the eyes of the sower. Paul accepted no discouragement – as we will see.

Precision

Paul letters were concise as writing materials were expensive and scarce. He chooses his words with precision; let's look at some of them.

"Great endurance" (v 4). Paul had endured troubles, hardships, distresses, beatings, imprisonments, and riots. However, it was not passive endurance, just putting up with what you cannot help. He could have helped it, if he had not gone where he did and preached what he did. It inevitably caused him trouble, but he accepted harsh experience as an aspect of his career. If it caused him distresses, then so be it. He never thought, "I can't preach because I might be lynched." He suffered stoning but took it as a hazard of his calling.

"Distresses." The Greek word that he used is *stenochoria*, inescapable circumstances, dire straits, not knowing which way to turn, with no room to maneuver. Psalm 18:19 speaks of God giving *"a spacious place,"* but Paul had no way out. He just had to stay and endure. He uses the same word later in his letter – *"difficulties for Christ's sake"* (2 Corinthians 12:10) – but this time his distress was not for himself, but for those who rejected the gospel. He also gave a clear warning to the Romans, using the same word: *"There will be trouble and distress for every human being who does evil"* (Romans 2:9). That kind of distress is avoidable – the very thing Paul wanted to save people from, even at the cost of his own distress. *"I could wish that I myself were cursed and cut off from Christ for my brothers"* (Romans 9:3). That is the pure heart of the evangelist.

> Leaders lead,
> but shepherds care.
> That is why
> the pastor theme
> dominates in Scripture.
> Leaders lead
> their flocks
> but shepherds
> watch their flocks.

Paul lists conditions in which he ministered: *"in beatings, imprisonments and riots; in hard work, sleepless nights and hunger"* (v 5). *"Sleepless nights"* is the Greek word *agrupnia*, meaning keeping one's self awake. Paul was not an insomniac; he was on the alert, even going without rest to care for people.

Caring for people often kept Paul awake. The word "care" (Greek: *merimna*) is used 5 times in this epistle. Care is not worry, but responsible concern. Paul did not sit around, waiting for people to consult him. He watched for their need and saw it when they did not, with the true heart of a shepherd.

Leaders lead, but shepherds care. That is why the pastor theme dominates in Scripture. Leaders lead their flocks but shepherds watch their flocks. The word *"leaders"* is used in Hebrews 13:17, but correctly it is those who are "esteemed": *"They keep watch* [agrupnia] *over you as men who must give an account."* They are to be held *"in the highest regard in love,"* says 1 Thessalonians 5:13.

They do as Scripture commands, being alert and *"always praying for all the saints"* (Ephesians 6:18).

Some do watch, but just for "something to happen," marvels, miracles, phenomena, or spiritual gifts. That is good, a sign of faith at least, but Paul watched for souls, somebody quietly wiping away their tears. A friend told me that while he was standing on the beach, a man ran past him, pushing him aside. He had seen a young man struggling in the water. No one else had noticed. He swam out to reach him, saved him, and laid him on the beach exhausted but safe. That is what the ministry is all about – noticing, saving, and doing what perhaps nobody else is doing. Filling a church, good meetings, pleasing an audience, yes, but also watching and caring. Our business is not business but people.

Paul's next words describe his personal attitudes. Do they describe ours? *"In purity, understanding, patience and kindness; in the Holy Spirit and in sincere love"* (v 6). These are not passive attributes that lie dormant within a person; they have positive outworkings. People can be tiresome, aggressive, feeble-minded, and boring, but he looked around at them, watching for the opportunity to do kindnesses. It sprang from one all-powerful attitude, "sincere love," "love unfeigned" (Greek: *anupokritos*). Elsewhere, the King James Version translates that word as "without hypocrisy" (James 3:17). Paul was not a mere religion pusher, a salesman with an ingratiating smile hoping for a big order. Nobody ever stood up and said, "Paul, you are not really like that!" We can fail to take account of this God-given example, thinking, "Well, that's just Paul isn't it?" No, it was not just Paul. He could have been very different, but he set himself to be what we know he was, motivated by genuine, sincere love.

> The lamp lit by the oil of the Spirit, never flickers. The man garrisoned by the power of God never flinches. Our calling demands no genius.

Of course, it is not always easy. For some it may be a temperamental struggle.

But there is help. Paul tells us the secret: *"in the Holy Spirit,"* not in our own stubborn spirit. Miracles like that are not wrought by human determination but by the Lord of all spirits, who changes our spiritual genetic coding. While the Holy Spirit does produce miracles that we can see, even more he makes us people of high quality concern and love, showing kindnesses and gentleness to everybody. Such qualities may be considered unsensational but they score high marks with God and make the world worth living in. That objective is inherent in evangelism and "sincere love" is an essential part of it.

Genuine ministry is *"in truthful speech and in the power of God; with weapons of righteousness in the right hand and in the left"* (v 7). Evangelism is a response to a cry for help – not to help ourselves, a chance to get somewhere or get something. It is not a profession but a rescue operation.

The world see through religious careerism, slickness, putting on the CD and letting the sound come out. Even the godless expect our speech to carry the ring of our own genuine conviction. No amount of eloquence or earnest straining and dogmatic intensity can make up for an uninspired heart that has no Holy Spirit anointing. The easy ploy, passionless careerism bores God – and man. Behind our spoken witness must be the solid reality of righteousness *"in the right hand and in the left"* – all round – arming us and disarming the unbeliever.

Paul's next words are an encouragement to us to keep on working for God through thick and through thin. This passage is so rich that it inspires me to read it over and over again. Here it is:

"Through glory and dishonor, bad report and good report; genuine, yet regarded as impostors; known, yet regarded as unknown; dying, and yet we live on; beaten, and yet not killed; sorrowful, yet always rejoicing; poor, yet making many rich; having nothing, and yet possessing everything." (2 Corinthians 6:8-10)

The world's attitude towards Christ and his true disciples is the Big Lie. It is led by the father of lies, the devil, and people follow *"the ways of the ruler of the kingdom of the air, the spirit who is now at work in those who are disobedient"* (Ephesians 2:2). In Roman times the Christians were grossly and falsely accused, even of cannibalism. Today misrepresentation of genuine faith is standard practice in the media. Christianity is represented as declining when in fact it is increasing faster than the birth rate. In this third millennium African people are turning en masse to Christ, slowly but surely changing the continent. World press policy is to maintain a conspiracy of silence.

The lamp lit by the oil of the Spirit, never flickers. The man garrisoned by the power of God never flinches. Our calling demands no genius, no great gifts. *"From the lips of children and infants you have ordained praise"* (Matthew 21:16). We *"stand our ground, and after we have done everything, stand"* firm in the truth, challenging an age built on the sinking sands of shifting opinions and uncertainty.

Questions

1. How could our ministry be discredited?
2. What is the difference between a "leader" and a "shepherd"?

CHAPTER 6

What use are the Stars?

*"Like your name, O God,
your praise reaches to the ends of the earth."*
Psalm 48:10

There is no such thing as good news until it is heard. *"Let everything that has breath praise the Lord!"* (Psalm 150:6). The word "gospel" – from the Greek word *euangelion* – suggests a public herald, as does the Bible word "proclaim" (Greek: *kerygma*). Tidings, news, had to be vocal in the days when there were no printing presses.

Universal Praise

Everything witnesses to God. That is what everything is for. *"The heavens declare the glory of God"* (Psalm 19:1). When Christians testify to Christ, they swing into the orbit of universal testimony that fills heaven and earth. *"All you have made will praise you, O Lord"* (Psalm 145:10). God's works advertise what he is. The unbelieving and unthankful skulk around outside; they do not belong to the purpose of creation. They relate to nothing and are of no significance (see Revelation 21:8).

Isaiah the prophet describes the mercies of God in two chapters, 43 and 44, declaring that God created Israel, redeemed and ransomed them, went with them through fire and flood, brought them together from afar, and will bring captives back from Babylon, make a way in the desert for them, and blot out their transgressions for one purpose, *"You are my witnesses"* (Isaiah 43:10). We do not witness about a God who does nothing or whose identity is confused. God means us to know who we are dealing with.

Bible witness is always clear, positive, and concrete. We know whom we are talking about. Paul said, *"I know whom I have believed"* (2 Timothy 1:12). John says, *"We do know that we have come to know him"* (1 John 2:3). He uses the word "know" 26 times in his three short epistles, but never the word "knowledge." Knowing God is personal and not at all the same as the knowledge of God. We witness to a God we know.

Psalms 146 to 150 call for praise to God in the heights of the sky, the sun, moon, stars, rain, animals, birds, trees, fish, and the roaring seas. This is praise to God their Creator but many know his greater work of salvation. Psalm 68:20 adds, *"Our God is a God who saves; from the Sovereign Lord comes escape from death."* In his vision of heaven, the apostle John heard the new song – one that is always new, the song of the Lamb.

We can picture the triumph train in glory. It is headed by redeemed singers, great phalanxes of the choirs of glory. Paul says, *"Thanks be to God, who always leads us in triumphal procession"* (2 Corinthians 2:14). He could have had in mind Psalm 68:11-35: *"The Lord announced the word, and great was the company of those who proclaimed it. Your procession has come into view, O God, the procession of my God and King into the sanctuary. In front are the singers, after them the musicians; with them are the maidens playing tambourines. The God of Israel gives power and strength to his people."*

Everything in heaven sings, *"Worthy is the Lamb, who was slain, to receive power and wealth and wisdom and strength and honor and glory and praise"* (Revelation 5:12). Distinguished people were there in John's vision and one of the heavenly "elders" said, *"These are they who have come out of the great tribulation; they have washed their robes and made them white in the blood of the Lamb"* (Revelation 7:14). Jesus said, *"In the world you will have trouble. But take heart!"* (John 16:33). Redemption is our exclusive theme, an inimitable contribution to the eternal symphony. Jesus said, *"You will be my witnesses"* (Acts 1:8). What he does for us sets all heaven on fire with joy and worship.

Paul uses another picture. *"We are to God the aroma of Christ among those who are being saved and those who are perishing. To the one we are the smell of death; to the other, the fragrance of life"* (2 Corinthians 2:15-16). The cursing and blasphemy of the un-redeemed is like halitosis, fouling the air, but praise and witness is the perfume of heaven, the scents of paradise. The holiness of Christ imparts cleansing and loveliness like the fragrance of the Garden of Eden.

Empowering Witness

If we experience salvation, it must show. *"Has the LORD redeemed you? Then speak out!"* (Psalm 107:2 NLT). In the beginning one thing amazed the pagans: the Christians themselves and their eagerness to convert others, even though being a Christian meant being a witness, a dangerous activity that could mean martyrdom. Believers held the fervent hope that Christ would soon return to fulfill the great purposes of the divine will. They warned everyone about it, seized every chance to speak out, and hurried to prepare the world for Christ's new age.

Today some witness, but some do not; even whole churches express no urgency about salvation. How can the world be impressed with their need of Christ when half the church shows no anxiety about it? The gospel cannot look very important if only a few church folk witness to it. Those few are ignored as unrepresentative fanatics. No amount of prayer and fasting, no efforts for ho-liness and power, can make up for a general neglect of witnessing, Christ's greatest command.

> No amount of prayer and fasting, no efforts for holiness and power, can make up for a general neglect of witnessing, Christ's greatest command.

Prayer retreats and rallies for revival can become mere occasions for fellowship. Prayers often throw the responsibility for souls back on to God, asking him to put spiritual "revival" pressure on them. That, however, is what he commanded us to do, for the *"gospel is the power of God for the salvation of everyone who believes"* (Romans 1:16). The Holy Spirit is the Spirit of witness; his great purpose is to empower witnesses. We cannot send the Holy Spirit out to do things. He only goes with us. He needs us to speak. Contrary to the popular saying, praying breath can be spent in vain. Praying is vain when it takes the place of witnessing. The New Testament exhorts us to pray for those who carry the gospel and for ourselves as we work for God, not for God to do the work himself. The Holy Spirit can only save souls through the word and *"faith comes from hearing the message"* (Romans 10:17).

It needs all Christians to speak up for Christ, from Bible Class teenagers to college theologians. God has ordained praise from the lips of children and infants for *"whoever offers praise glorifies me"* (Psalm 50:23 NKJV). Psalm 148:3 instructs the silent stars to declare God's glory by their shining existence, but we can do better than the stars. They have no mouths, no tongues, and no language, but we are articulate, with the gift of speech with which to glorify God.

The best evidence for the gospel is witnesses themselves, so much so that it qualifies for divine help. We need to be Spirit-baptized to be his fellow-workers. *"You will receive power when the Holy Spirit comes on you; and you will be my witnesses"* (Acts 1:8). It fulfils Psalm 138:1-3: *"I will praise you, O Lord, with all my heart; before the 'gods' I will sing your praise. I will praise your name for your love and faithfulness; for you have exalted above all things your name and your word. You made me bold and stout-hearted."*

Christ died and he lives to save precious people; he is always close to his witnesses. They are his friends, instruments of his saving power, agents, and representatives on earth of him in glory.

We should bear some likeness to him by his Spirit even though we are human and imperfect. We are his temples and *"in his temple all cry 'Glory'"* (Psalm 29:9). To glorify God is not an optional hobby. Witnessing justifies our existence. To make his goodness known for ever gives us divine purpose. Through us God will ultimately fill the universe with the knowledge of himself, what he is, a God of infinite love, mercy, and goodwill. To glorify himself, he first draws us to himself and then teaches us to rest in him, living examples, demonstrations, of his salvation.

Everything is for God, including ourselves. That should be our motivation – to be something for him. God is all and in all, so that his Son Jesus did everything he did to glorify the Father. He said that the death he would experience would be for the Father's glory. At the end Christ will hand over even his kingdom to God (1 Corinthians 15:24). Witnesses may work as church publicists, social workers, or doctrine promoters, but their motivation has to be to glorify God and their experience of salvation is their in-spiration. Believers are Jesus' people. He owns us. We rejoice in him. *"We do not preach (about) ourselves, but Jesus Christ as Lord"* (2 Corinthians 4:5).

Witness is testimony to our fellowship with Jesus. His messengers are his confidantes, his friends. We speak out of that relationship, all about Jesus. Scripture focuses on him. He did not bring good news; he was the good news. Mark's first words are *"the gospel of Jesus Christ"* (Mark 1:1). Jesus is the word preached, *"the gospel of his Son"* (Romans 1:9). The core message is Jesus: *"I resolved to know nothing while I was with you except Jesus Christ and him cru-cified,"* wrote the apostle Paul (1 Corinthians 2:2).

Many who believe that all roads lead to God like rivers lead to the ocean are deceived. This begs the question, "All roads lead to what god?" Jesus said, *"No one comes to the Father except through me"* (John 14:6). Why is that? Because he alone showed us the Father. Knowing what the Father is, no road leads to him except Christ

Jesus, who is the Way. Jesus alone revealed him to us and he alone knows the way to him. Other gods are totally different, distinct from the Father. The way of Christ simply cannot lead to Allah. The Hollywood Star Wars films call God "the Force." How can he be found? There are a hundred million Hindu gods. What road leads to them? Buddhists have no god; their road leads to oblivion in Nirvana. The Christian road does not lead to oblivion for Jesus stands waiting to receive us. Some 500 years ago the Sikh Guru Nanak put together a patchwork of his own ideas of God. You get to his God by mystical means and prayers and by taking on Sikh identity. The Christian road is not even on the same map.

The gospel is the declaration of Christ on the cross rising from the tomb for our sins, and it provokes praises. Yet witness is more than praise. The word praise occurs some 200 times in the Palms and 100 times in the rest of Scripture. God calls it *"my praise."* In fact, the whole Bible rings with praise, revelation and witness to the Father and the Son honoring God's majesty, but the gospel is the scheme of eternal redemption, saving power and grace. It is testimony, teaching, doctrine, the overture of God and his instrument of reconciliation with the rebellious world.

The wonderful Unfolding

Witness is not a leisure-time interest but the fundamental objective of life. Jesus witnessed to himself. That is so significant. *"The Pharisees challenged him, 'Here you are, appearing as your own witness; your testimony is not valid.' Jesus answered, 'Even if I testify on my own behalf, my testimony is valid. In your own law it is written that the testimony of two men is valid. I am one who testifies for myself; my other witness is the Father, who sent me"* (John 8:13-18).

Those Jewish leaders knew the Scriptures, that in them God testified to himself. They perceived that Jesus was doing the same thing, ranking himself with the Father. God has to reveal himself to us or we would never know him. We would never find him by seeking for him unless he steps forward. Jesus was unknown on earth until he showed forth his glory and testified to himself. We stand with him and point to him

All the teaching of Jesus turns inward to himself. Many times he used the divine title of self-revelation, "I am!" Only God can reveal God. He is the light of the world but, like John the Baptist, we must *"tell everyone about the light"* (John 1:7 NLT).

> The gospel is the declaration of Christ on the cross rising from the tomb for our sins, and it provokes praises.

He made a profound and surprising statement: *"No one knows the Son except the Father, and no one knows the Father except the Son and those to whom the Son chooses to reveal him"* (Matthew 11:27). This seems mysterious but we can understand one thing, that only Jesus has shown us the Father. *"If you really knew me, you would know my Father as well."* (John 14:7). Who shows us the Son? That is the work of the Holy Spirit: *"He will bring glory to me by taking from what is mine and make it known to you"* (John 16:14-15).

God witnesses to himself in the Scriptures. Look at its beginnings. In Genesis he reveals himself as the Creator and the Friend. In Exodus he is the deliverer; in Leviticus the Holy One; in Numbers the shepherd; in Deuteronomy the covenanting God; in Joshua the promise-keeper; in Judges the defender; in Samuel the God who speaks; and in Kings and Chronicles the King of kings. What he is progressively unfolded throughout the 39 books of the Old Testament. God spoke slowly because people could not take it in any sooner.

Finally came the wonderful unfolding in Jesus the Lord. He came out of hiding, and we are called to point to him, joining the glorious concourse of proclamation, of our Lord Jesus and his eternal love, the joy of all heaven. Jesus gives it all such a personal touch – *"You will be my witnesses"* – and we should be proud of that!

Questions

1. We can witness without prayer or pray without witness.
   Do you agree?
2. We can witness with our lips without being a witness.
   Can you explain that from what you have read in this chapter?
3. Everything is for God's praise but Christians are special.
   Can you say why?

CHAPTER 7

People are human

"He who has the Son has life."
1 John 5:12

Why God sent Evangelists?

What is life all about? The future shape of history was once menaced by a craving for cucumbers. The Bible records the epic of Israel flinging defiance in the face of Pharaoh and walking out of his prison house of slavery under his very nose. They were beginning a revolution with profound global effects that are continuing now in the third millennium. Then, unbelievably, they wanted to go back and surrender to their old captors. Why? For Egypt's fresh salads and cucumbers!

Trivialized life is modern enough. The Guinness Book of Records lists dozens of pitiable ambitions and worthless achievements. The applause of fame is heard today for brainless "records" such as glutton pork pie swallowing and speed drinking. Television gives public approval to celebrities eating live creepy crawlies. The popular press gives prominence to men drinking pints of beer upside down and putting ferrets inside a man's trousers. It reduces life to stupidity and encourages a casual view of human dignity that could be a factor in the river of bloodshed polluting the fair earth. The most famous are the least great today.

A good time is often reduced to a binge and hangover. Stomachs become beer kegs and alcoholics satellites to a whisky bottle; millions are obsessed by sex, money, or drugs. Life so often amounts to nothing and if some think about their end, it is with the hope that when the day is done, it will "be all right on the night."

It is a mystery to me, but many people never even open the Bible. As if it were infected with anthrax, they never handle it. Yet beyond all argument it is the happiest book in the world and the key to a full life, vitality, and effectiveness. God did not make us bored. He is the fountain of life. He created all true joys and pleasures, but not so that we could be independent of him. Jesus talked of the prodigal son using his father's money to get away from him to a far country where he shared food with pigs. Away from God is that far country. People who were designed to be temples of the Holy Spirit are picked up sick and drunk. Born for transcendent glory, they are fed up with life. Created as companions of the Almighty, they become pals of the uncouth and blasphemers. That is why God sent evangelists. He also sent evangelists because everyone faces adversities that fall like snowflakes, icy and chilling, and we all need the mantle of God's love wrapped around us.

We are exhorted to *"preach the word"* (2 Timothy 4:2). It is life's bedrock. However, modern doubts leave some preachers without the word, scavenging for topics just to say something. They dignify this no-gospel talk by calling it "life preaching," relevant. Without the word, it is no more than personal opinion, ideas about life's "problems." Complaints have been made that chapel services have been more like trade union meetings; congregations that gather for worship have to listen to social views and prejudices.

Preaching anything that happens to pop into one's head as a word from the Lord is just not good enough. Having listened to a new preacher, a lady once said with some relief, "The Lord prevented him from saying anything ridiculous."

Nevertheless, our business is not with heavenly sunbeams, but with people on planet earth who are *"born to trouble as surely as sparks fly upward"* (Job 5:7). Charles Spurgeon commented that some preachers seemed to be addressing the gas brackets not the occupants of the pews. True hope and encouragement come from God. To win souls we must win people, human beings with inescapable human concerns.

Religion is not God's only interest. His creatures in his own creation must always be under his review. The great secret of the Pentecostal-Charismatic revival is that it is not a spiritual faith only; it also has physical and material aspects. The Spirit of God makes our bodies his temple and manifests himself in physical signs, mortal life joined to the immortal Spirit. "We feel the throbbing of immortal life grow stronger as the days go by," as the old hymn says.

Handbook of Life

The gospel's eternal-quality life should show. When we are born again, we need only be what we are, for we have *"the right to become children of God"* (John 1:12). We *"put on the new self"* (Ephesians 4:24). *"Work out your salvation with fear and trembling, for it is God who works in you to will and to act"* (Philippians 2:12). Act out the Christ-life. We were crippled but Jesus said, "Walk!" … and we can – so we had better! Birds fly, fish swim. They can do those things because they were made that way. Believers can be the children of God because they are "made that way."

> Birds fly, fish swim. They can do those things because they were made that way. Believers can be the children of God because they are "made that way."

There are many kinds of ministry. At present a "prophetic ministry" is in vogue, usually predictions about individuals present in church services. Actually, the prophetic ministry in the Old Testament was only 3% prediction and otherwise concerned the ways of righteousness. Jesus said, *"The poor have the gospel preached to them"* (Matthew 11:5 NKJV) – they did not have their fortune told.

Jesus' ministry gripped ordinary non-religious folk. His Sermon on the Mount (Matthew chapters 5 to 7) shows why. He dealt with real issues: law, murder, adultery, divorce, oaths, worry, revenge, enemies, love, poverty and charity, food and clothing. The NIV headings list all the points.

We are not born at our own request, but we are born again when we ask. It is a divine operation. God wants us to want it and God wants those who do want it. Whoever believes receives.

The Bible is a handbook of life, dealing with every imaginable area of mortal existence. It contains useful guidance for warriors, widows, the weak, and the wealthy. It has wise things to say, actions to recommend, comforts to indicate. The Psalms express the full range of human emotions from depression to jubilation. It gives us a new focus and perspective, as if projected onto a screen from the divine angle. The authors of many Psalms were greatly distressed but poured out their grief in wonderful examples of trust in God.

The word relates everything to God. Without him our years on earth end as rags and tatters swinging in the wind and the greatest of world events make no greater mark than ripples on the surface of a pond, their noise and clamor become lost echoes. With God, however, even the insignificant becomes significant; a cup of cold water assumes everlasting importance. We matter to him and following his instructions gives us a profound sense of meaning, whatever we do: *"Whatever you do, whether in word or deed, do it all in the name of the Lord Jesus. Whatever you do, work at it with all your heart, as working for the Lord, not for men"* (Colossians 3:17,23). All duties and concerns have a place in his cosmic schemes.

The gospel gives a new interpretation to the chapters of the human story. Modern novels reflect modern life, clueless about God. They break off unfinished as episodes without meaning or objective. That is what life is like today. However, in God's book, the Author and Finisher brings together the incidents and accidents to make providential sense. He shapes the stresses and strains to perfect the plot and bring it round to what he wants it to be. *"We are God's workmanship"* (Ephesians 2:10).

A friend recently showed me his ornamental aquarium and explained how the exotic fish need special food and conditions but, first of all, water! Our own existence also depends on many conditions but, first of all, we need God; without him we flounder like fish out of water. Like breathing, God has no alternatives. God has no stand-in, no deputy. *"Whoever believes will be saved, but whoever does not believe will be condemned"* (Mark 16:16).

Everybody lives, but what sort of life do they have? That is the great concern of evangelism. Jude talks about souls that are *"twice dead, uprooted"* (v 12). Paul wrote that some are *"dead even while they live"* (1 Timothy 5:6). They breathe and walk but their eye has no vital spark.

Life without Christ is artificial. Drink, drugs, and other kinds of "life" are crutches for crippled lives, zest from a bottle. Revelation 3:1 says, *"You have a reputation of being alive, but you are dead."* In contrast, Paul testified that he was *"dying, and yet we live on"* (2 Corinthians 6:9). Believers have life and live without needing a rave-up to have a good time.

Without God, we are defective, not being made to be without him. That is the gospel message. Evangelism restores what is lost back to its original design. The dry bones in Ezekiel's valley of vision *"came to life and stood up on their feet"* by the word of the Lord (Ezekiel 37:10). The word of the gospel repeats that miracle in reality, setting the fallen and morally crippled upright on their feet. Christ in the heart is real, not a passing emotion. His life is in us like the blood in our veins even when we do not feel it. Evangelism gives us life. It is resurrection. *"You he made alive, who were dead in trespasses and sins"* (Ephesians 2:1 NKJV).

True "life preaching" is eternal life preaching. Without Christ, all other kinds of life, the prosperous life, busy life or whatever are wasted kinds of life. Authentic life is eternal life, the greatest change since Creation. *"Whoever believes in the Son has eternal life, but whoever rejects the Son will not see life"* (John 3:36). No higher form of life has ever been conceived.

"Eternal life" means more than for life for evermore. It is a code word for a new thing. Until Christ came, nobody had any notion of what it was. The expression "eternal life" had to be explained. It means a quality of life too rich ever to deteriorate. I will explain more about it in a moment, but it is nothing less than the Lord wrapping us in his mantle. Nothing can imitate or reproduce it. It cannot be valued by any normal standard except by its price tag – the life of Christ himself and the horror of the cross.

Life of the eternal God

God's gifts are usually given freely. He sends the rain on the just and the unjust without being urged to do so. *"You open your hand and satisfy the desires of every living creature"* (Psalm 145:16). However, the gift of new life in Christ comes by asking. We are not born at our own request, but we are born again when we ask. It is a divine operation. God wants us to want it and God wants those who do want it. Whoever believes receives.

Eternal life is not a shot in the arm to boost our natural experience. It is not mind power, an "up-rush from the subconscious," but a down-rush from God. Religious practices and mind power may stimulate natural strengths, drawing on our personal reserves, but eternal life is a totally fresh resource. *"Our Savior, Jesus Christ, has destroyed death and has brought life and immortality to light through the gospel"* (2 Timothy 1:10).

Museums have workshops for cleaning and restoring masterpieces, but the artists would never touch up their pictures; they only paint new ones. Scripture tells us that *"we are his workmanship"* (Ephesians 2:10) and God does not do a repair job on us: *"In Christ Jesus neither circumcision nor uncircumcision means anything; what counts is a new creation"* (Galatians 6:15).

Religions lay out a road map or religious comfort, competing with one another as they do so. The gospel is not a road map but the delivery point of life. That is brought out in two main Bible words, the Greek *zoe* and *bios*, both meaning life. Natural life is *bios* but *zoe* can be seen as supernatural, life from God, and is a great theme in the New Testament, where *bios* is mentioned only 10 times while *zoe* occurs 135 times. God created life for Adam, for all animals, flora and fauna, and even for angels. However, when Scripture says *"in him was life"* (1 John 1:1), it means that it was always there, never created, God's own endless life. John the apostle spoke of Christ on earth saying he had touched the word of life. Jesus was the Word of life, original *zoe* life, manifested in physical form, God incarnate. *"The eternal life has appeared to us. We proclaim what we have seen and heard"* (1 John 1:2).

Now that is the life bestowed upon the heirs of salvation. They *"participate in the divine nature"* (2 Peter 1:4). We receive eternal life, which is the life of the eternal God. The whole glorious and unspeakable richness of God, whose disposition is pure and unceasing joy, his quality of life is given those who believe in him.

Jesus told people what it meant to have eternal life: *"I have come that they may have life and have it to the full"* (John 10:10). Elsewhere, *"to the full"* is translated *"more abundantly"* (KJV).' This *"more abundantly"* is used over 100 times in the New Testament to mean "abounding," "exceeding," "more," "some left over," "increasing," "in superabundance." It is characteristic of everything God does. He has no scales on which he measures out his gifts. He simply fills his hand and opens it over us.

It troubles us to think that animals, trees, and even fish live longer than we intelligent breathing humans. It seems out of order and it is. The balance must be somewhere, and that is in "eternal life." We were meant to outlive all other living things by the gift of eternal life. True life is in two stages, on earth and in heaven, much as a dragonfly begins in water and then flies in the air.

At great cost God has begun the process for us. Death ends only the physical stage, and then our personality continues in a wider dimension with wider consciousness.

God has a master plan for the heirs of salvation who *"participate in the divine nature"* (2 Peter 1:4). He has breathtaking purposes in our fragility and brevity. We are exposed and tested in every way. We could perish, overcome by the world, the flesh and the devil, but by divine grace we overcome them. *"God chose the foolish things of the world to shame the strong"* (1 Corinthians 1:27). We were made for his glory as we are to walk through the dark valleys of life and through great tribulation. We, the weakest of creatures, are intended to be *"more than conquerors"* (Romans 8:37). His life breaks through in us.

God's strategy was for himself to share our weak estate, coming to us as a babe in a mother's arms. He overcame evil in its most aggressive forms, not by might, power, brute force, or destruction, but by love, light, and life, by his gentleness towards sinners. Here I have touched on the truth about the future of Gods' creation, God's ultimate purposes in all the worlds there ever might be. The sons of God are a new order in creation, redeemed and born again with eternal life.

Our Destiny opens up

We had no say in our first birth, but for our second birth we call on Christ. He accepts us when we accept him. *"To all who received him, to those who believed in his name, he gave the right to become children of God – children born not of natural descent, nor of human decision or a husband's will, but born of God"* (John 1:12-13). We can opt in or opt out. This is the golden light in our earthly sky. *"How great is the love the Father has lavished on us, that we should be called children of God! And that is what we are! What we will be has not yet been made known. But we shall be like him"* (1 John 3:1-2).

Those who "belong to a religion" keep up certain customs and often wear certain attire; they point to it saying, "That is my religion." Christians have nothing like that to display. They have eternal life and that is their only display. *"The kingdom of God is not a matter of eating and drinking, but of righteousness, peace and joy in the Holy Spirit"* (Romans 14.17). The Christian sign is not physical, yet not invisible. It is love. Jesus left only one command, to love God and our neighbor. We are as much Christian as we love. Without love we are not of God but the gospel renders love as possible. *"We know that we have passed from death to life because we love our brothers"* (1 John 3:14). His love, not our loves, saves us. *"God has poured out his love into our hearts by the Holy Spirit"* (Romans 5:5).

Working for God, even working miracles, does not save us. We are not saved by defending God or by trying to save the church. God defends us and saves us by the church. We need him. Eternal life is a gift, not an achievement. *"Whoever lives and believes in me will never die,"* Jesus declared (John 11:26). *"Through Jesus the forgiveness of sins is proclaimed to you"* (Acts 13:38). Our sin is expunged, *"every mountain and hill made low"* (Isaiah 40:4), all iniquity buried in the divine forgetfulness.

Jesus put so much of what I have written here into one story (Luke 15). A father had a waster for a son. Yet when that son returned home, his father was beside himself with joy. The

> The Christian sign is not physical, yet not invisible. It is love.

worthless son had tramped home, dusty, unwashed, in rags and stinking of the pigsties. But his father ran out to meet him, kissed him, embraced him and brought him into the home with feasting, music and dancing. *"Your brother has come,"* he said to the elder brother, showing how much he loved them both. However, for the elder son, the young man who had returned home was an object of contempt; he referred to him as *"this son of yours."* I noticed how the father, an old man, ran to greet his son. That is Christianity.

One of the foundation Bible stories is the Exodus of Israel from Egypt. Moses led it, and said, *"Blessed are you, O Israel! Who is like you, a people saved by the Lord?"* (Deuteronomy 33:29). But even more special than Israel is a born-again, blood-washed believer, "saved by the Lord." Jesus himself saves us: *"I, even I, am the Lord, and apart from me there is no Savior"* (Isaiah 43:11). Christians are not clones of one another, mass produced on a factory belt, each put together according to the same formula; each one is a new creature, an act of God the Creator.

Our destiny opens up. We are the tools of God to make a new heaven and a new earth. We are nothing less. We have eternal life in Christ. We are the people of the future.

Questions

1. What practical issues did Jesus address in his Sermon on the Mount?
2. What does this chapter tell us about the nature of "eternal life"?

CHAPTER 8

Being super good

"You who are spiritual."

Galatians 6:1

Slippery Places

The phrase "spiritual man" is found in the Bible letters to Corinth (1 Corinthians 2:15). What is a "spiritual man"? People initiated into the early Greek mystery religions called themselves spiritual. They boasted of their "spiritual" knowledge. Paul takes their expression up and uses it in a clearly different context to describe people who have received the Holy Spirit and walk in the Spirit.

The most important person in any church is the one who knows God the best – the spiritual man. In Galatians the apostle did not instruct leaders or pastors to restore the erring man or woman; he instructed the spiritual (Galatians 6:1). Then Paul surprisingly warns the spiritual man to be watchful, for he also can fall (Galatians 6:1). Psalms 35 and 73 and Jeremiah 23:12 talk about *"slippery places."* It refers to the limestone rocks common in that part of the world which become slimy and slippery when wet.

We all can fall. There is no such place as one where it is one hundred percent impossible to slip. Salvation does not mean Jesus forgives us and then leaves us to it. There are three tenses: he has saved us, does save us and will save us. He saves us, holding our hand as we walk on the brink of the abyss, or we would slip over the edge.

Let me say something of my long experience about pitfalls on the path. The Psalms often talk about snares and traps, even pits, prepared for the unwary.

One of the slippery places for a leader is adulation. People often make idols of their spiritual leaders. Praise is a heady wine to be accepted only in a very small glass. Gulped down, its intoxication can deprive us of our wits and we soon head for a fall. A nursery rhyme describes Humpty Dumpty sitting on a wall and falling off. The wall was safe, but he was not and "all the king's horses and all the king's men could not put Humpty Dumpty together again"! David lamented over King Saul, who said, *"I have acted like a fool and have erred greatly"* (1 Samuel 26:21) and over Jonathon, his fine son. David wept, *"How are the mighty fallen!"* (2 Samuel 1:19).

Jude 24 says God *"is able to keep you from falling."* God can keep us upright, so it is doubly sad when the mighty fall as I have seen happen. Paul's evangelist companion Demas was a Humpty Dumpty. He seemed to be safe when working so close to Paul the greatest apostle, but the apostle reported that Demas *"because he loved this world"* had forsaken him (2 Timothy 4:10). Even one of those chosen to be Christ's own 12 disciples, Judas Iscariot, ended up in an epic historical disaster. The ancient temptations that have felled many mighty men – money, power, fame and sex – are still pouncing on the unwatchful. Drawn aside by the magnet of this present world, they lose everything worth anything.

Christ's Temptation

It is hard to imagine Jesus being tempted, but the Bible tells us that *"He has been tempted in every way, just as we are – yet was without sin"* (Hebrew 4:15). This has been misread as if Christ experienced every possible temptation known to man, even homosexuality, as an Anglican bishop dared to suggest. However, *"tempted in every way"* is qualified by the addition of the words *"just as we are"* and nobody is ever tempted with every possible sin. We are not all tempted to react violently, to steal, to lie, to defraud people, or to commit adultery, but we each have our own besetting temptation. The devil sees to that. Christ's testing related to his own unique life and salvation purpose. They were real tests that only he could experience, not the temptations of everybody on earth, but the pressures were as acute. Jesus faced the same dilemmas, had to make decisions in a world of a thousand options and uncertainties, as we all must. His perfect attitude of love was his wisdom and righteousness. Because he came through these rock-strewn and treacherous seas, he can guide us too.

Satan tempted Christ by telling him to prove who he was. It seemed so plausible, so right to assert his deity. He had the power, why not use it? It would silence every mouth, every critic, and every kingdom would acknowledge him. Turn stones into bread – yes, he could do that. Fall from a tower and not be hurt – he could do that, too. Put on a demonstration of omnipotence – no problem. But Jesus chose not to do any of those things.

In fact, what Satan asked is what everybody wants today – let God prove he is God. Why leave it open to doubts when by a single act God could be proved for ever? Well – a single act? There has already been more than one! For us creation is enough! And if it is not, Christ rose from the dead! He made bread when the right time came, with the right motive. He manifested his deity when the right time came, after he had suffered the horrors of a crucifixion death. Yet as

> God did not make us so strong that the devil could not get at us. It is God's plan for us to be weak. We are conquerable but never conquered while he is with us.

he himself said, people would not believe in the ultimate of all wonders that some one should rise from the dead.

He did rise from the dead, he is risen, but it did not and does not compel the world to believe. The heart of man is desperately wicked. There is no possibility of "hard evidence" of God's reality having any impact, if people refuse to believe in God. Jesus said, *"Blessed are those who have not seen but yet have believed"* (John 20:29). Believers know what he meant – that blessing is supremely great.

Hebrews 4:15 says that Christ can sympathize with our weaknesses. That is a striking statement. Did Christ have weaknesses to overcome? He said, *"The Spirit is willing but the body is weak"* (Matthew 26:41). He did overcome. His flesh would naturally shrink from the appalling torture that he knew lay ahead of him. His temptations were real, not mere theatre. We all shrink from death. That is a universal weakness, and as he faced death in the garden of Gethsemane, he prayed, *"Not my will, but yours be done"* (Luke 22:42). Christ *"tasted death for everyone"* (Hebrew 2:9). But he conquered for us, and drew out the fangs of fear. That gives us a tremendous witness. What a gospel to preach! *"We face death all day long (but) in all these things we are more than conquerors through him who loved us"* (Romans 8:36,37). Overcoming temptation and the devil is not a rare miracle for believers but their whole way of life. Just being a Christian means being a conqueror from the first moment.

> Pride is all about hugging ourselves because we are what others are not or have what others do not have.
> Pride is like a cat through the door - in before you know it.

When we are tempted we feel it as a weakness, as if it were wrong to feel tempted, and we are ashamed of ourselves. We need to realize that it is not wrong to feel tempted, unless we dally and flirt with the idea. We can *"take captive every thought to make it obedient to Christ"* (2 Corinthians 10:5). It is a case of wearing the helmet of salvation on our head (Ephesians 6:17). We must not boast of being strong, for we are all weak. Big macho men are known to have "a strong weakness," getting into a rage, for example, like children in a temper tantrum.

God did not make us so strong that the devil could not get at us. It is God's plan for us to be weak. We are conquerable but never conquered while he is with us. *"God chose the weak things of the world to shame the strong"* (1 Corinthians 1:27). He made us that way, and our weakness is nothing to be ashamed of, for it is the factor by which God can prove his strength. The devil targets us with his darts, but God allows it as an opportunity for us to discover divine power. If we were so inherently strong, untouchable, able easily to shrug off the tempter, where would be the glory of the victory? *"My power is made perfect in weakness"* (2 Corinthians 12:9). The man who thinks he is too strong to worry about the devil will awake to a bitter morning of disillusionment. The arm of flesh will fail. Our reliance is on the mighty arm of the Lord. Our turning to him is the very thing he wants.

The Comforter does not come to make us comfortable. God has other objectives beyond our comfort. We ourselves are important to him for those objectives. Through us he can demonstrate his glory. He can exploit every temptation, the world, the flesh, and the devil, and make our weakness take on glorious muscle to ride like horsemen across the face of the devil.

The enemy sees Christ's witnesses as dangerous. He will try to engineer their downfall. He goes about looking for those he can devour, especially the most active and effective witnesses. Yet God gives grace to help in time of need. He made Daniel too tough for the lions.

Pride

Pride is subtle, the vice that seeps into our attitudes like water into a leaking boat. On his island, Robinson Crusoe was never proud because nobody was there that he could outdo! Pride is all about hugging ourselves because we are what others are not or have what others do not have.

By contrast, the kind of pious sentimentalism that renders people so humble that they lose all self-confidence is not part of the Christian make-up, far from it. We admit that we are sinners but Christ lifts up our head. He takes us from the dunghill to sit among princes.

Pride is like a cat through the door – in before you know it. We can even be proud of being humble, confessing to pride with smugness. Someone said that he knew his friend was very humble because he told everybody about it. We try to be humble only if we think we are great. The truly humble do not need to try to be humble – they just are, like Jesus. Jesus never tried to be humble. He did not wash the disciples' feet as an exercise in humility. Popes have washed the feet of beggars to show they were humble! All it showed was how condescending they were. Jesus washed feet as if it were second nature to him, like smiling.

It takes no powers of penetration to discern pride in others, but gestures can also be mistaken as motivated by pride. A man is not showing off at all with a $100 if he has a $1 million in his wallet. Self-respect is not self-conceit. Without some self-esteem our morale sinks to despair. Between proper self-regard and fancying ourselves as superior, the line becomes very thin. We fantasize. Paul wrote, *"In humility consider others better than yourselves"* (Philippians 2:3). This, he says, was the attitude of Christ Jesus – the very nature of Christ, not his pose. There is a word, originating from the Greek, for the attitude of heart that breeds condescension: *hubris* – "excessive pride or self-confidence." A preacher once said that it was the word for "the insolent arrogance which forgets the essential creatureliness of the condition of being human." [1] The Lord appointed pastors, apostles, teachers, and evangelists to do a job, not to exalt them as a superior class of people.

Christ did not pretend, putting on mock humility. He knew who he was for *"he did not consider equality with God something to be grasped"* (Philippians 2:6). We can recognize our worth, our skills, our wealth, even our genius without putting on airs and graces. Paul had to affirm himself but it was not "swank." He said that the false apostles boasted which forced him to the same detestable necessity, but he proceeded to describe his sufferings as a true apostle (2 Corinthians 11). If we have ten talents it is wrong to act as if we

---

[1] Expository Times N° 115, page 422.

had only one, but it is just as wrong to flatter ourselves about having them, for God gave them and we did not create them. We can develop what we are, but cannot be what we are not. A bird is not proud that it can fly. We cannot be proud that we can do what we do, for God created us that way. We may as well boast because we can breathe.

Pride shows up when we become indignant and self-defensive, ruffling our feathers if anyone makes a remark about us. It is worth listening to their comments. There might be some degree of truth in defamation, and we can turn criticism to our advantage – if we are humble enough.

The problem of being a critic is that it expresses superiority. We may know more or know better than others but to put it into words needs lowliness of mind. Motivated by prejudice, a critic will twist facts, exaggerate, quote his victim out of context, express contempt, and vilify someone whom he has never met just to hurt them, even in the name of God or "truth." It is the forked tongue of a venomous serpent. I have a fear of joining the accuser of the brothers, the devil. Some have declared themselves to be my enemies but I do not see them as they see me. They are lost souls who need salvation, and need the word of love in Christ Jesus as spoken through me. If we destroy others, we will end up destroying ourselves.

The Holy Spirit does not bless our work in order to feed our vanity nor anoint us to earn applause. Do we serve God in order to be noticed? It is a poor Christian show when we upstage others. Admiration is not the reward of our service to God and should not be our motive. Nonetheless, we all need

> The Holy Spirit does not bless our work in order to feed our vanity nor anoint us to earn applause.

encouragement, appreciation and assurance, or our spirit wilts. People are shy about praising others, mainly for fear of sycophancy, flattery to win favor. The world is full of jealousies and cynicism but among Christians there should be openness of heart. *"Rejoice with those who rejoice"* (Romans 12:15) – be glad of one another's success. One man's victory in the gospel is everyone's victory. Evangelists vying against evangelists provide the devil with source of amusement.

The word "pride" in the New Testament is *alazon*, originally a name for bragging charlatans, comic figures in Greek dramas. A Christian believer who sets out to impress with his greatness, exposes himself to ridicule. The apostle Paul said, *"I am what I am by the grace of God"* (1 Corinthians 15:10) but he still insisted on his apostleship, still spoke of what he did, and suffered even in some moving passages in his letters. In 1 Corinthians 13 he describes love. What we know of Paul exemplified the great thirteenth chapter of the first letter to the Corinthians. He never boasted of himself, but always of Christ. He portrayed himself as dwarfed alongside Christ's greatness. *"He loved me and gave himself for me"* (Galatians 2:20).

> Courage is not the absence of fear; it is its conquest. The Psalmist said, "When I am afraid, I will trust in you". That is the antidote to fear.

Paul expressed pride in being a Roman citizen, a Hebrew of Hebrews, a citizen of "no mean city," meaning Tarsus, which had a population of about half a million and was Roman (Philippians 3:5, Acts 21:39). At the end of his life he could rightly "boast" that he had fought a good fight, although he said it as a challenge to Timothy (2 Timothy 4:7). Paul was not self-deprecating. Personalities who say "I am a very humble person" are slimy characters. We are workers for God, the most honorable service in heaven or earth and our working clothes are humility – *"God opposes the proud but gives grace to the humble"* (1 Peter 5:5).

Fear

Everyone has some fear to hold them back and the great hindrance to all witness for Christ is fear of man. Everybody experiences a tremor of fear at one time or another. Fear can make cowards of us all. You feel scared, and others do too, but they still witness and bring people to the Lord. In my campaigning I might have great fears because I have received many death threats. Assassins have been sitting only yards away from me when they have been arrested with their guns in hand. However, I am afraid to fear, for it would show lack of trust in God.

David seemed fearless when he tackled Goliath, but the Psalms of David show that he had the same feelings as everybody else. *"Ungodly men made me afraid"* (Psalm 18:4 KJV). His adrenalin set his heart beating faster when he realized what he had let himself in for, facing this great nine foot of a man, but his eagerness against a foe whom he regarded as the enemy of the Lord, overcame every apprehension. Dare anything for God!

Perhaps Paul's statement in 1 Corinthians 2:3 is not fully appreciated: *"I came to you in weakness and fear and with much trembling."* We find it difficult to picture that valiant apostle breaking so boldly into uncharted paganism with the gospel message but admitting to fear, trembling and affliction. Courage is not the absence of fear; it is its conquest. The Psalmist said, *"When I am afraid, I will trust in you"* (Psalm 56:3). That is the antidote to fear.

Actors in the theatre say that nervousness adds vibrancy to their performance. In witness, if you are nervous, it does not matter if it shows. People are more impressed when they notice that it is not easy for you to approach them. It would have been like that when the Corinthians first saw Paul. They saw him trembling, unwell (possibly with malaria, some suggest, his thorn in the flesh, a very common illness in those times with no cure), and they probably admired his dauntless attitude and some took him to their heart.

"Have no fear of sudden disaster, for the Lord will be your confidence" (Proverbs 3:25-26).

David had a friend called Jonathan, the son of King Saul who was David's enemy. A situation arose where, for David's sake, Jonathan had to risk his father's anger. David was concerned about how Saul would react to Jonathan: *"Who will tell me if your father answers you harshly?"* (1 Samuel 20:10). In modern English, he might have said something like, "Your father might get angry with you. What then?" The King certainly did answer Jonathon *"harshly,"* trying to skewer him with a javelin. Any true friendship may call for being "answered harshly," and serving our Lord could well produce some harsh answers from others. Does it matter? Queen Esther went into the king's presence venturing to approach the emperor in person and said, *"If I perish, I perish"* (Esther 4:16). If the first Christians, who became confessors and martyrs, had listened to their heart and how fast it was beating, we would not be hearing the gospel today. He who hesitates is lost.

Spirituality

Jesus said, *"Apart from me you can do nothing"* (John 15:5). In fact, we can do things without him, but not in the way he meant. We can do things, but cannot achieve much on our own. He explains why, using the image of a vine with branches: *"No branch can bear fruit by itself; it must remain in the vine. Neither can you bear fruit unless you remain in me"* (John 15:4). We can look wonderful, so efficient, like the fig tree Jesus saw in full leaf; it looked really good but had produced no figs. Unfortunately, the Church has fruitless branches. Unless we stay in him and the life sap of the Spirit flows through us, we shall be fruitless because no learning, no sophistication and no eloquence can ever take the place of the Holy Spirit.

At Mount Carmel the priests of Baal laid a sacrifice quite correctly and put a great deal of energy into the effort to spark it into flame.

Elijah also built an altar, laid a proper sacrifice, and the fire fell. We have excellent organizations, wonderfully crafted sermons and erudition, and nothing to be criticized. The question might still be: where is the fire? Our service for God is needed as part of the process. The Holy Spirit provides the vital igniting spark of new life.

To be pre-occupied with church work and have no time for Jesus makes us like Martha serving Jesus but leaving him sitting there on his own until Mary kept him company. King Ahab was confronted by a prophet over his negligence in battle; the prophet talked about a soldier losing a prisoner whom he should have been guarding. *"While your servant was busy here and there, the man disappeared"* (1 Kings 20:40). That was the prophet's parable of Ahab's failure as king. Church service keeps us busy while the real job is not getting done. A witness or evangelist should be a man of God not just a busy man. Even Jesus himself took time to talk to his Father.

> Integrity is being what you should be when no one is watching, being real with ourselves, honest in our minds, for *"as a man thinks in his heart, so is he".*

A survey found that many ministers spend only a few minutes in prayer and read the word only to find sermons. Is that "remaining" in Christ? Not the man talking about God, but the man walking with God is God's man. We can cocoon ourselves with work so that God cannot get through to us and looks elsewhere for special help.

On the other hand, what God wants you to do is obvious, and it does not need God to detail you off every morning. If you listen with a blank mind, you will hear all kinds of voices. God does not wait to speak until we have a "quiet time." He can and will ring the bell at any time, and we do not need to be super-sensitive to heavenly promptings. When God has something particular to say and we are generally willing to hear what he has to say, then it is his responsibility to make sure we hear him.

Integrity

This is a testing word. Integrity is being what you should be when no one is watching, being real with ourselves, honest in our minds, for *"as a man thinks in his heart, so is he"* (Proverbs 23:7 NKJV). Some believe that the angels in heaven hear our thoughts. Well, if that were so, how would we feel? Have we secret sins? *"Whatever is lovely, think about such things"* (Philippians 4:8). Without integrity of heart we will despise ourselves as grubby and despicable, instead of noble. *"You desire truth in the inner parts; you teach me wisdom in the inmost place"* (Psalm 51:6). If we preach what is right and do what is wrong, we are mere stage actors. Shame will come as sure as the dawn.

The great temptations have always been in the same realms, summed up as "the world, the flesh and the devil." Mammon is the name for money, or for the world regulated by money. Our life is to be regulated by the love of God, not the love of the world or money. The flesh brings carnal desire. The letter of James says that we are tempted by our own desires (James 4.1). The devil can leave the world and our own fleshly hankerings to do their own work.

The main satanic ploys are sins of the spirit; that is, pride, hatred, envy and love of power. Jesus condemned sins of the spirit more than sins of the flesh. Today we do the opposite. Church leaders allow members to go on for years not speaking to one another, bearing grudges, harbored wrong attitudes in their hearts, but they come down very hard on the sins of the flesh.

The world can corrupt us with fashion, loose morals, prejudiced attitudes, consumerism, encouraging us to compete in affluence, showing off our houses and possessions. Wrong motives and self-interest can creep in – the little foxes that spoil the vines (Song 2:15). The disciples followed Jesus but still wanted prominence. Even when he was talking about his coming passion, they were jockeying for position. James and John hankered for privilege,

wanting the best throne seats with Jesus (Matthew 20:21). Church
life has always been an arena for Christians seeking notice and jealousies arise over the smallest offices.

Church leaders are vulnerable to the desire for power. People look
trustingly to them and pastors can be tempted to excess authority, acting as cult leaders, *"lording it over those entrusted to them"*
(1 Peter 5:3). Only Jesus is Lord. He does not make little lords,
little masters. As he said, there is only one who is our Master –
he himself (Matthew 23:8). Some arrogate to themselves lordship
over people, interfere with the private and home responsibilities of
church members and make decisions for them in totalitarian fashion. Jesus himself was Lord but never dictated to his disciples in
such matters. Shepherds are not sheepdogs, and church folk are not
dumb animals. Psalm 32:9 says, *"Do
not be like the horse or the mule, which
have no understanding but must be con-
trolled by bit and bridle."* God gives us all
wisdom. The Lord on high gave us pastors but not bosses to order us around.

> We must work
> as if it all depended on
> us and pray as if it all
> depended on God.
> We should see the
> masses as Jesus saw
> them with tear-dimmed
> eyes of compassion,
> willing to humbly
> serve them.
> This is the will of God
> for us all.

These are likely dangers coming from
the world, the flesh and the devil. In previous chapters I have stressed zeal, faith,
the Holy Spirit and other qualities of
true Christian service. The Lord has no
second army in reserve. We are all in the
field with no fail-safe plan, only us. We must work as if it all depended on us and pray as if it all depended on God. We should see
the masses as Jesus saw them with tear-dimmed eyes of compassion,
willing to humbly serve them. This is the will of God for us all.

Question

Of the pitfalls listed in this chapter, which do you consider the
most dangerous?

Part 2

*Christ redeemed us
from the curse of the law by becoming a curse for us.
He redeemed us in order that the blessing given to Abraham
might come to the Gentiles through Christ Jesus.*

Galatians 3:13-14

CHAPTER 9

The cursed Mob

"The large crowd listened to him with delight."

Mark 12:37

A French aristocrat in pre-revolution times exclaimed, "Me, not go to heaven? Nonsense! I am a lord!" He surprised nobody then. The famous and rich were always considered God-chosen, even from Roman times, and kings were held as awesome, super-humans whose very touch could cure diseases. The commoners were virtually the litter in the streets. Even up to a century or so ago in England the poor were considered the great unwashed. Churches built mission halls for them as upper class people did not want them in their nice chapels.

Social pride has always existed, though changes radically affect the present day. In the early twentieth century in Great Britain "working class" people "knew their place," and there were even higher and lower-ranking servants. Maids and others "in service" in great houses were never to be seen by the family for they were substrata. The two world wars began to erode class distinctions and many factors began breaking down the traditional walls of inequality.

In another country, Jesus was born into a world of rigid class divisions that are difficult for us to appreciate today. Half the people in the world were slaves with no rights whatever, acquired like shop purchases and as easily expendable. Even Israel had class divisions within the religious community. If the robe of a higher placed chaber brushed against a member of a low order, he would consider himself defiled.

A revolutionary Faith

The disciples set out to change that world. They remembered, for instance, that Jesus had been talking to crowds of peasants and laborers, whom he saw as wandering around like *"sheep without a shepherd"* (Matthew 9:36) and they observed his compassion for them. Jesus had called God their Father. They learned that believers of all races and classes were equally precious as the children of God.

Christians are often persecuted, being charged with radical attitudes. Christianity is a revolutionary faith that champions the oppressed and claims freedom and respect for all people. We see everyone as precious, each one a "died-for-by-Christ" person, special in God's sight. They are his people, acquired at the frightful cost of the blood of his Son. In Christian circles some leaders are known to "lord it over those entrusted to them" (see 1 Peter 5:3) but they have no inherited right to do that. Jesus never dictated to his disciples in their daily lives, nor did he delegate authority over men and women to anyone.

Jesus' heart embraced everyone, bringing hope to forgotten people. *"The crowd listened to him with delight"* (Mark 12:37). Jesus gave them recognition whereas the authorities saw them as "the mob." They poured out of their little homes to be with him. Jesus was their man, their friend, the Good Shepherd. He had come to them seeking the lost and befriending the friendless when no one else cared. The Jerusalem authorities were scared. He was imparting a new spirit of self-worth and dignity as children of God. He planned to make even a common fisherman a "somebody," a fisher of men, a leader.

In Israel the "mob" could make neither head nor tale of the functions of the professional religionists, their rituals, and legalistic religious observances, such as tithing even the salt on their table. Although those men were fussy about such minor details, they showed cold indifference to the spiritual state of ordinary people.

Proud of their religious superiority, they looked down on the rest, declaring, *"This mob that knows nothing of the law – there is a curse on them"* (John 7:49). Tragically, the crowd themselves believed that they were indeed cursed, while the religious leaders believed that they were the elect. The fact that they, too, were sinners escaped their notice.

The despised strata were *"the people of the land"* (Jeremiah 1:18), who had no instruction in Mosaic Law. They had joined Jews returning from the Babylonian captivity 500 years earlier and Ezra the priest ruled that as they were not pure blooded Jews they were excluded (Ezra 10:11). They offered to help build the Jerusalem temple but were refused (Ezra 4:1-4). So the Samaritans built their own place at Mount Gerizim, in Samaria. Their bruising rejection created permanent animosity, but these were people whom Jesus loved. He went to Samaria, found the most unlikely person, a much married woman living "in sin," and turned her heart to God. She was a sample of his new order of free children of God. He later also told an immortal story from which we have the common phrase "a good Samaritan". He even mentioned Samaria in his last words, the Great Commission, commanding that they should be the first non-Jews to hear the gospel.

Lifting the Curse

Christ told John the Baptist, *"The good news is preached to the poor"* (Matthew 11:5), to the untouchables, the outsiders. The crowds *"were amazed at his teaching because he taught as one who had authority, and not as their teachers of the law"* (Matthew 7:29). He went to the deprived who could give him nothing, and that is a salutary lesson for today. Our own CfaN African campaigns attract the poorest people in the world and we remember Christ's first recorded teaching, *"Blessed are the poor in spirit for theirs is the kingdom of heaven"* (Matthew 5:3). In his first synagogue sermon Jesus quoted Isaiah 61:1: *"The Lord has anointed me to preach good news to the poor."*

Whether we are thanked or not, the world owes us thanks when we preach the gospel, regardless of who hears it. Without the gospel everyone is poor. Wealth and affluence are only pall bearers for those dead in sins. Without Christ, what is there in the end? Simply nothing, only substitutes. Nothing ever done, said or written can take the place of our message of the crucified redeemer.

Paul declared that he was set apart for the gospel of God (Greek: *euangelion*). That word is made up of *angelia* – a message – with the prefix *eu* – good. Change it and it is neither good nor a message. Haggai 1:13 reads: *"The people obeyed the voice of the Lord their God and the message of the prophet Haggai, because the Lord their God had sent him. Then Haggai, the Lord's messenger, gave this message of the Lord to the people"* (Haggai 1:12-13).

Christ lifts the curse, as Scripture predicted. After the flood, Noah cursed Canaan for his sin, as Cain was cursed in the beginning. In contrast, God blessed Abraham. Part of that blessing was the promise of the land of Israel, but Canaan's cursed descendants occupied the land, and it was known as Canaan before Israel entered it. Abraham only moved around in Canaan in Bedouin style and owned nothing except what he purchased. He had with him his nephew Lot, a far less godly man. Lot chose to live where *"the Canaanites and Perizzites were also living at that time"* (Genesis 13:7). But Abraham kept clear of all Canaanite influence, in accordance with God's plan.

The curse of the Canaanites became awful reality when Joshua invaded Canaan. However, God's promise to Abraham was *"All peoples on earth will be blessed through you"* (Genesis 28:14) – which produces the extraordinary situation in which the cursed people were to be blessed, their curse cancelled.

The blessing of God was not going to be just nice vibes; everything would be better, a new order of mortal existence introduced. Beyond everything else would be salvation in Christ, the Son of

Abraham canceling every curse and malediction ever uttered. *"Christ redeemed us from the curse of the law by becoming a curse for us. He redeemed us in order that the blessing given to Abraham might come to the Gentiles through Christ Jesus"* (Galatians 3:13-14).

The reality of curses and blessing is illustrated in a strange episode in Christ's ministry (Matthew 15:21-28). Jesus made a surprising journey to the northern Gentile area of Tyre, a two or three-day walk. Soon after he arrived, a Canaanite woman began clamoring for attention, asking Christ to help her daughter who was tormented by an evil spirit. The disciples tried to send the mother away and asked Jesus to tell her to go, but she flung herself across his path and begged him to deliver the girl. Noting her astonishing faith, Jesus set the daughter free from the curse of the demon – but not before he had demonstrated an enigmatic reluctance to listen to her. Then, when he did listen, he remarked that he had been sent only to the lost sheep of Israel. Why did Jesus respond like this? The whole story is like a stage setting.

First, Jesus acted in recognition of the curse on Canaanites, while presenting himself as the woman's hope. He had been sent to Israel, the heirs of the blessing of Abraham. The Canaanite woman represented the ancient curse of Canaan. She herself was aware of the ancient racial tensions and ironically spoke of her people as *"dogs,"* which is how Jewish people then might have spoken of them. The old situation of cursed Canaan was rearing its head. Yet that is the very reason why Jesus went to Tyre. It explains the whole episode. The purpose of God was that in him, through Abraham, all peoples would be blessed. History is played out here. Jesus first recognized the Canaan curse and then expelled the evil spirit and with it, the curse. That demon represented the curse, and Jesus demonstrated his authority to break the ancient curse and to substitute God's blessing for it. Jesus breaks every fetter. As for Canaanites generally, Jesus included one in his 12 apostles: Simon (Mark 3:18, Matthew 10:4).

Crossed over

When Israel journeyed to Canaan, God promised to drive out the Canaanite idolaters as with hornets (Exodus 23:28). At the end of his career, Moses gave a recital of their long journey. In Deuteronomy he recounted how they passed through enemy lands, and (in chapter two) he used the Hebrew word *abar* 12 times. It is translated to "cross over." "Cross over" is a Biblical code word for salvation. Abraham "crossed over" the river Euphrates when God called him out of Ur. Israel crossed over the Jordan. Jesus crossed over the brook Jabbok on his fatal last journey. To become a Christian we "cross over" from the kingdom of darkness into the kingdom of God. In secular language, we "cross the Rubicon." We cross over *"from the power of Satan to God"* (Acts 26:18). There is no compromise, no sitting on the fence, no keeping a foot in both camps – both feet are in the kingdom of God, wholly the Lord's.

The tragedy of Lot was that he left Ur of the Chaldeans with Abraham, but settled down with the Canaanite people. As time went by he came close to sharing their curse. Only the prayers of Abraham and a visit by angels rescued him from the destruction of Sodom, Gomorrah and the other cities of the plain. He lost everything, including his wife, and was left with only his two incestuous daughters.

The picture tells us a lot. Conversion means leaving the world behind to cross over into the kingdom of God, into a new state of life. We are new creatures ready for the new world, the city of God which has foundations. Without Christ the world has no future.

Believers have crossed over into the kingdom. They bear kingdom characteristics. Different cultures and races are always noticeable from their accents and the way they behave; kingdom people likewise bear the evidence of kingdom culture. The world is suspicious of anything so different, strange and new. New people attract mockery. If Christians suffer persecution, it is an honorable recognition of their heavenly citizenship. It is a distinction of which they can be proud.

Isaiah spoke of God's people *"soaring on wings like eagles"* (Isaiah 40:31). Eagles are the feathered kings of the air. They know how to live and move where earthlings cannot, in the environment of the thermals, the *pneuma* of the earth. The people of God live and move in the environment of the Spirit, the *pneuma* of God. People of the Spirit know how to live in the Spirit. They breathe his qualities and it shows through. That is an essential element of evangelistic witness – kingdom people are different.

During civil war in Israel, Jephthah fought against Ephraim and trapped them at the fords of the Jordan. The Ephraimites had to "cross over" the ford but Jephthah told each man crossing over to say, *"Shibboleth."* The Ephraimites could not pronounce that word; they said, *"Sibboleth."* It seemed a small distinction but it was revealing. Their enemies knew them immediately and did not let them cross over (see Judge 12:1-6).

In the end Christian believers cannot be hidden. Voltaire, the French atheist philosopher, said that he could not believe in the redeemed because they did not look redeemed. What a stupid remark! What did he think redeemed people would look like? Would they wear haloes? The evidence does not need to be a display of supernatural pyrotechnics. *"We have this treasure in jars of clay"* (2 Corinthians 4:7). Millions of believers are humble, undistinguished, perhaps old, perhaps ungifted – not likely to make the newspaper headlines. We remain ordinary human beings; the difference is that we know God and he works changes in us that unbelievers do not see or appreciate.

We are linked with God in the name of Jesus. After Moses died, Joshua led the people into the land of promise as a type of Christ, the *"captain of our salvation."* Joshua's name was Oshea or Hoshea, meaning "salvation" and Moses added the prefix *Je*, part of God's name (Jehovah), making it Jehoshua, "God is salvation." We render it in English as Joshua. In its Aramaic form it is contracted to Jesu or Yesu, which is Iesous in Greek and Jesus in English. It signifies freedom in a large place, unfettered by restrictive rules. Christ is salvation. We are saved "in him," as in the cleft of a rock.

For many in Israel religiousness showed only in their costumes and proud duties. Jesus was a thorn in their side, wanting reality, not religious ostentation. He exposed their religious showmanship and they sent their police to arrest him, but his words arrested them and the police came back without him, saying, *"No one ever spoke the way this man does"* (John 7:46). The word "man" here is *anthropos.* Their meaning was "No mere human being ever spoke like this man."

The temple authorities dealt with religion, but only for the interested. The gospel is not designed for merely religious connoisseurs, or anyone who happens to like that sort of thing. The gospel is for the *"far off,"* the unworthy and those who know they are unworthy. *"Blessed are the poor in spirit,"* Jesus said (Matthew 5:3) – that is people who think nothing of themselves. The gospel is needed by everyone as much as they need water and light.

Water is offered in all kinds of drinking vessels. One person will accept it in a cup and another in a jug, but water can also be offered in a vessel from which people will not drink. Preachers can all be very different characters. We can put people off. We need wisdom. God made us different to reach different people. We are vessels for God. The divine potter made us on his wheel for the special purpose he had in mind but, whatever we are like, we are intended to carry the water of life to the thirsty people of this world.

Surveying the scene at that time, Paul said that not many mighty or noble people were called. Several of the apostles were only fishermen types. Modestly, Paul did not mention himself. God had placed him among them with his brilliance and fame. The appeal of Jesus is not to undistinguished people and no others. Men of note went to him, like the ruling Sanhedrin members Joseph of Arimathea and Nicodemus. Jesus referred to Nicodemus as *"Israel's teacher"* and Nicodemus referred to Jesus as *"a teacher who has come from God"* (John 3:10,2). John tells us, *"Many even among the leaders believed in him"* (John 12:42).

Prince and pauper have the same human needs, air, food, light … and the gospel. However, they respond to different calls from different people. A young doctor attended a service conducted by D. L. Moody and was about to leave because a man was praying an unending prayer. Then the evangelist said, "While our brother is ending his prayer let us sing a hymn." The young doctor liked this frankness, stayed, gave his life to Christ and became a medical missionary to Labrador. He was Sir Wilfred Grenfell who founded a work comprising hospitals, medical ships, nursing stations, orphanages and cooperative stores, and who wrote about 24 books. For his extensive work he was knighted by King George V. God put him in Moody's meeting at the right moment to experience the incident that struck just the right chord in his character.

Some will "hit the sawdust trail" but others would never go near a tent meeting. We must do what we can in all the ways we can. God orders things his own way and will call people of every kind, small and great.

> We must do what we can in all the ways we can. God orders things his own way and will call people of every kind, small and great.

Paul was well acquainted with the famous Greek thinkers in Corinth. He asked, *"Where is the philosopher of this age? Has not God made foolish the wisdom of the world?"* (1 Corinthians 1:20). Athenian intellectuals confessed themselves ignorant of God. Well, yes, because thinkers never agree with one another, never reach finality, never come close to the idea of salvation, and have never imagined anyone like Jesus. We have their famous writings and we can see how right Paul was.

When Paul confronted these intellectuals, he did not argue about their ideas, but pointed to Christ risen from the dead, a single positive message, not a philosophy. Christ is a fact not a controversy. The truth had come to that pagan centre. Paul came to them, as he did to the Galatians, suffering in some way from "a thorn in the flesh." They were not impressed by his physical presence or eloquence. But the power of the gospel broke through, even because of his handicap. They loved a man who would come to them, trembling, weak, and so absolutely on fire with his faith. Witnesses do not need personality to win people with personality. The weak can win the strong and the little people win the great. A little girl talked about what God could do. She was a slave girl and cared about her master. It brought about the most notable healing of sickness in the Old Testament, Naaman's cure of leprosy.

God does not use pretentious people trying to impress others with their brilliance or greatness. Being what you are not is off-putting or distracting. If we are sincere, not show-offs, our faces will show it. "Putting on an act" is fatal to your purpose.

You do not need a blinding, hypnotic presence to proclaim the word of God; you need to be yourself, without artificial gestures or a special preaching voice. Just be what God intended you to be, your honest self, God's servant. God wants people like that to bring comfort and edification and to feed the sheep. *"Do your best to present yourself to God as one approved, a workman who does not need to be ashamed and who correctly handles the word of truth"* (2 Timothy 2:15).

Questions

1. Why did Jesus seem so glad that he preached the gospel to the poor? Don't we all do that?
2. How did the apostle Paul deal with the intellectuals of Greece?

CHAPTER 10

The blessed Bedouin

"He sent him to bless you."

Acts 3:25-26

Who first preached the gospel? The answer is found in Galatians 3:8: *"God announced the gospel in advance to Abraham: 'All nations will be blessed through you.'"* That was four thousand years ago.

God was full of joy about sending his Son to save us, and seemed impatient to tell people about it, as if he could not keep it a secret. The coming of Jesus into the world meant so much to the Father. In the earliest Bible books God constantly drops hints about him but keeps his name a secret. By his providence, the Lord somehow wove the story of Jesus into the story of Israel. Those Old Testament books speak of Jesus.

God's Search System

God declared clearly what the good news was when he preached it to Abraham, namely, his determination to bless all nations. That is God – from his first dealings with anyone. It was a heavenly invasion, unsought, a sign of his spontaneous goodwill. No one had prayed for him to bless them. In fact, no one had prayed or had any idea of anybody blessing them. Their superstitions and gods never rose beyond a hope of good luck. The world was a place of accidental and unpredictable circumstances, beyond their control, and they felt like bits of nothing dealt with in the most casual manner by the mighty forces of nature around them.

Despite what people might think, God's intention when he made man was to bless him. Right at the start we read, *"God created*

> By definition, religion is about seeking God. Religion is a search or approach system with God as the elusive object. In Scripture God seeks us. Christ established a search system or road map to God.

man, male and female, and God blessed them" (Genesis 1:27-28). He loved the world. Blessing people was God's own idea. We only ask God to bless us because he said that he would, anyway. We would not have thought of it ourselves. Nothing is said about Abraham seeking God at any time, and certainly not before the time when he was in Ur of the Chaldeans. In that area they knew God only as a supreme god above all the others. Abraham called him *"El Elyon," "God Most High."*

With his approach to Abraham, God began to take a hand in world history, to change it. "God moves in a mysterious way his wonders to perform," the poet William Cowper wrote. In this instance he began to affect the world by taking one man, Abraham, out of it into a tent in the wilderness.

Four centuries later God made a new overture, offering the hand of friendship to Moses, a prince of Egypt. Psalm 103:7 tells us that *"he made known his ways to Moses."* This spontaneous coming of God to people is the wonderfully distinct feature of true religion. We are told several times that *"the Lord spoke to Moses,"* where the Hebrew word for "speak" means personally, not as if speaking to a stranger.

By definition, religion is about seeking God. Religion is a search or approach system with God as the elusive object. In Scripture God seeks us. Christ established a search system or road map to God. The Bible cuts across our natural inclinations and thoughts. God approached the first man on earth, Adam, and when Adam fled in shame in the Garden of Eden, God came calling, *"Adam, where are you?"* (Genesis 3:9). Jesus always did what the Father did, and said that he had come *"to seek and to save what was lost"*

(Luke 19:10). That golden thread links every Bible page, God pressing his goodwill on human beings, with outspread arms of care, undertaking provision and life-fulfillment.

Today the gospel is still the same joyful news as 2,000 years ago. The first few men who dared to follow Jesus found themselves swept into the greatest enterprise ever promoted. They were honored, as we are, too, if we do what they did. The privilege is open to us.

God's Parameters of Blessing

God made a covenant with Abraham. It was not an agreement or contract but an unconditional undertaking; the conditions were only that Abraham trusted God to do what he said. *"Abraham believed the Lord and it was credited to him as righteousness"* (Romans 4:3) – that is, as qualified for God's favors. Life can strain relations but the Abraham's covenant of blessing depended on God's good will, not Abraham's. Abraham made bad mistakes. His descendents did ten thousand times worse, but God has never gone back on his covenant. Often Israel stepped outside the arena of God's blessing and even sought blessing or help from idols, but God was faithful to his undertaking.

The blessing of God is the legacy of everybody that is born, but the world generally fails to "buy" into it. In fact, we all step outside the parameters of his blessing, being sinful, until he comes seeking us, his hands loaded with love gifts. We make fools of ourselves, but God never renounces his covenant. Five centuries or so after God covenanted with Abraham, *"God remembered his covenant with Abraham"* (Exodus 2:24). He suddenly confronted another dubious character, Moses, to implement his word.

The everlasting covenant that God made with Israel promised earthly and material benefits. He made Abraham rich, and did the same for Isaac and Jacob, Abraham's son and grandson, and preserved their ways. His blessing covered the entire landscape of their lives, family and health. God never goes back on his word, and God has never reneged on what Abraham understood and tested as God's blessing: *"No matter how many promises God has made, they are 'Yes' in Christ"* (2 Corinthians 1:20). He said, *"I tell you the truth, until heaven and earth disappear, not the smallest letter, not the least stroke of the pen, will by any means disappear from the Law until everything is accomplished"* (Matthew 5:18).

Nevertheless, Christ Jesus came to give us higher expectations than material comforts. Many factors obviously will affect our circumstances of earthly gain but his will and covenant are steadfast. He taught us to pray, *"Your will be done on earth"* (Matthew 6:10) for that does not often happen. Christ's great priority was to bring in eternal salvation, the greatest of all blessings, a "package deal" containing all goodness.

The Gospel of Blessing

For centuries the church had no clear teaching on miracles other than as extra events outside normal religion. Miracles were performed only by men and women whom the church regarded as "saints." A saint was someone who practiced excessive austerity. Before the Catholic Church today declares someone a "saint," evidence is needed that they had performed a miracle. If they had brought healing to anyone then it was accepted that they were holy saints. They had a surplus of grace which they had accumulated by their rigorous lifestyle. Only an extremely good man could heal.

The shadow of this idea still lingers among Christians generally. A physical sign is often taken as something that is achieved by extraordinary spirituality, a sign of much prayer and fasting, for instance. A physical manifestation is looked upon as the peak of God's presence. That is not what Scripture teaches. A miracle is a gift of God by faith: *"Does God give you his Spirit and work miracles among you because you observe the law, or because you believe?"* (Galatians 3:5).

A miracle is not beyond normal Christian experience; it is part of it. The benefits of God in the gospel are not purely spiritual, as some would like us to believe. Scripture does not contain a wisp of a suggestion that the gospel is a substitute for the hundreds of physical promises. It is true that *"he has blessed us in the heavenly realms with every spiritual blessing in Christ"* (Ephesians 1:3), blessings which were not known until Christ completed his work, but no way does it suggest that all other promises are cancelled out. God did not reduce his goodness to spiritual matters only and withdraw previous forms.

Human beings are flesh and blood and God does not treat us as pure spirits. He knows our frame, that we are dust. He meets us as earthly humans with earthly needs. Our occasions of trust in God arise predominantly in our physical state. The ancient promises of God always linked forgiveness with healing. All his promises are *"'Yes' in Christ"* (2 Corinthians 1:20), including bodily healing and material goodness, which in fact are specifically mentioned.

The gospel is basically the fulfillment of God's promise to Abraham to bless all nations on earth, that is, with the same blessing as Abraham whose prayers brought healing to a whole clan of people. Any "gospels" that do not reflect that first gesture of God do not fully represent the whole range of Bible truth. The gospel of Christ is the same as the gospel that God preached to Abraham but with the added spiritual dimension. When preaching to the Jews, Peter said, *"You are heirs of the covenant God made with your fathers. He said to Abraham, 'Through your offspring all peoples on earth will be blessed. When God raised up his servant, he sent him first to bless you"* (Acts 3:25-26). That is how several English Bibles read but the Greek makes it even better. Literally, it is God sent him *"blessing you."* He scattered his blessings as he came.

> A miracle is not beyond normal Christian experience; it is part of it.

Jesus came blessing people to the very end of his days on this planet. When Jesus was last seen, *"he had led them out to the vicinity of Bethany, lifted up his hands and blessed them. While he was blessing them he left them and was take up into heaven"* (Luke 24:50-51). His hands were lifted in the gesture of blessing as clouds drifted over his presence. Then heaven's messengers assured the watching disciples, *"This same Jesus, who has been taken up from you into heaven, will come back in the same way you have seen him go"* (Acts 1:11). *"In the same way"* means with his hands raised in blessing. Those hands are still raised in blessing. He is absolutely the same Jesus – *"Jesus Christ is the same yesterday and today and forever"* (Hebrew 13:8).

Now comes the strange thing. When Christ was raised from the dead, the disciples were more troubled than cheered for a while. The Lord had appeared to them and they knew that they needed him and that to lose him was unthinkable, even impossible. Then, 40 days later, they saw him disappear out of their sight. That could have been the greatest heartbreak possible. But Luke writes, *"They returned to Jerusalem with great joy. And they stayed continually at the temple, praising God"* (Luke 24:52-53). How could they do that? Because Christ blessed them as he parted from them and it was real, not just a sign.

That is the gospel, the gospel of blessing first revealed to Abraham and then to Moses: *"He made known his ways to Moses"* (Psalm 103:7). The message has always been misinterpreted and that is the enemy's primary work, deceit, even from the times of ancient Israel. God gave them the Ten Commandments without a penalty attached to any of them but a clear promise attached to at least one. Israel and most of us have shunned their guidance. Originally inscribed on stone, they were symbolically smashed by Moses as he saw Israel dancing around an idol.

Moses knew God better than as a God of fury and judgment; he asked God, *"Show me your glory"* (Exodus 33:18). He asked because he did not know what God's glory was. God showed him. *"And he passed in front of Moses, proclaiming, 'The Lord, the Lord, the compassionate and gracious God. Slow to anger, abounding in love and faithfulness, maintaining love to thousands, and forgiving wickedness, rebellion and sin'"* (Exodus 34:6-7).

His glory turned out to be more than a show of splendor. His glory is his graciousness and gentleness. A dozen or more times in the Old Testament we read of his *"his tender mercies,"* though only twice in the New Testament is that expression used. Did Israel know only too well that God was a great heart of kindness? Did they presume upon his longsuffering? Maybe we should note that Israel never heard of hell until Jesus came. He was the supreme manifestation of divine love, but he it was who made the clearest reference to judgment and hell. God's penal judgment is real, and it prompts his own answer, the gospel of redemption.

The gospel message itself is not a message of judgment. Reading the sermons of Paul and Peter and the epistles of others shows us that they could hardly be called hellfire preachers. Most people are already fearful of what lies beyond death and the gospel is good news because it is the good news of sins forgiven, hell subdued and peace with heaven. The apostles preached hope to an age without any hope at all. They did not build Dante-like pictures of an infernal torture chamber filled with screams of anguish. *"God did not send his Son into the world to condemn the world, but to save the world through him"* (John 3:17). The world was self-condemned and its own sin was already a bitter harvest: *"Jews and Gentiles alike are all under sin"* (Romans 3:9). We are *"condemned already"* (John 3:18). Judgment is present and also lies waiting ahead.

Jesus was perfectly aware of that. His titanic efforts to save us from judgment speak for themselves of the dreadful reality of dying for our sins, cut off from God. Our nature depends on God, and without him our very nature perishes. A lost soul is like an uprooted tree fallen on the ground, rotting. Such a fate for sinners drove him to extreme measures, causing him to tear himself from eternal glories and descend to the grubby village of 2,000 years ago and then to the cross. There he submitted to the hell of our deserts in penal substitution. He shielded us from the sword of God by interposing his own body. His gospel was – and is – hope salvation and blessing.

Going back to Abraham, we read in Genesis 24:1: *"Abraham was now old and the Lord had blessed him in every way."* That is a useful statement. God's blessing is not just nice feelings. It is *"in every way,"* life's corridors filled by divine care. Time goes by and God's blessing fosters a deepening personal relationship with him, which is greater than all imaginable material benefits.

> Salvation is not an offer in the bargain basement. God did not just speak and it was done, like making trees. He bled for it.

The blessings of God come with salvation. Salvation is not an offer in the bargain basement. God did not just speak and it was done, like making trees. He bled for it. It cost too much for easy grabbing, just there for the asking; there was much more to be gained than could be achieved by reciting some glib "only believe" formula. God's blessing is vast, taking in life and eternity. He is hardly likely to bestow his passion-bought goodness on anybody for the sake of a glib and casual, "Thanks, I'll have it!"

There is no separate blessing package. It is offered with all Jesus did for us, part of his operation for our lost condition. The blessing of God begins with the word of the gospel and repentance and the Holy Spirit's work. Nothing less than the passion and resurrection of Christ are involved, passions translated into our experience of salvation. We receive forgiveness or nothing at all. *"He who did not spare his only Son – how will he not also, along with him, graciously give us all things"* (Romans 8:32). God's blessings come only with the gift of Christ.

Before even God could help us, the matter of sin and its soul-blighting effects had to be cleared. We quoted elsewhere the Galatians text about Christ bearing our curse on the tree (Galatians 3:13). It looks back to Deuteronomy 21:22: *"Anyone who is hung on a tree is under God's curse."* That text seemed so odd and arbitrary. Nobody understood why a hung man would also be cursed. It was an inspired word, put there for one man, Christ himself, who hung on a tree with nails though his hands and feet. *"God made him who had no sin to be sin for us"* (2 Corinthians 5:21).

Blessing cannot be had without due process as part of God's package deal. We reject the old life and receive Christ and his blood-bought salvation with the gift of eternal life. Without that work, demanding anything from God has no safe grounds. The blessing of God begins with the unspeakable gift of Christ. That is blessing, the greatest of all blessings. With him, we are freely given all things.

God has blessings that he pours freely on everybody without being asked. He makes his sun to rise and his rains to fall on the just and the unjust, the godly and the ungodly. Unthankful though the world is, God is faithful. But he is not casual. His greater gifts are available only to those who ask. They are for those "in Christ." Kingdom benefits are for those in the kingdom. The blessings of God are so comprehensive and he is so great-hearted in generosity that the world takes advantage, is thankless, avaricious, and materialistic. We may gain the whole world, for God is so gracious, but lose our soul. Heaven's blessing turns into a curse for the faithless who grow fat on God's goodness.

The story of Israel in the wilderness is like a parable. They had no faith in God's care. They murmured in discontent about the food that he provided, demanding flesh to eat. God gave it to them and they devoured it greedily and made themselves sick. The comment of Psalm 106:15 is: *"He gave them what they asked for, but sent a wasting disease upon them"* or, as the KJV puts it, *"He gave them their request, but sent leanness into their soul."*

The gate to the field of God's blessing is at Calvary. Many bypass that holy place and jump the fence to gain temporal advantage but lose eternal life. Without salvation nothing in the entire world is a true blessing. But the Christian sings:

> *Christ is my meat, Christ is my drink,*
> *My medicine and my health;*
> *My portion, mine inheritance,*
> *Yea, all my boundless wealth.*
> *I've found the pearl of greatest price,*
> *My heart doth sing for joy*
> *And sing I must, for Christ I have,*
> *O what a Christ have I!*

Questions

1. Does God ever bless unbelievers?
   If so, what does he do for them?
2. On what grounds does God work miracles?

CHAPTER 11

A new Incantation?

"In the name of Jesus."

Acts 9:27

"In the name of Jesus" is not a magic formula. Saying words – even Bible words – is an empty formality unless … That "unless" is what we will consider in this chapter.

The first reference to the name of the Lord is in Genesis 4:26: *"At that time men began to call on the name of the Lord,"* which simply means that prayer and worship began as a common practice. In later years, when the Jewish rabbis taught Israel, the name of God – YHWH (Yahweh or Jehovah) – was held as so awesome that only one man ever uttered it, the High Priest of Israel, once each year on the Day of Atonement. He entered the Holy of Holies carrying fire concealed in incense smoke and sprinkled blood 7 times before the ark of testimony and the mercy seat as part of the high priestly ritual. At the most solemn moment he spoke the holy name and vast crowds of worshippers fell prostrate on their faces. That name was so great that a Jew would not step on a piece of paper in case the name was written on it.

A Jewish sect at the time of Christ, the Essenes, who were stricter than the Pharisees, had a small community at Qumran in the sun-whipped area of the Dead Sea. Their rules were found a few years ago in the Dead Sea Scrolls; they laid down that any member of the community using God's name at any time and in any place would be expelled.

In our modern Bibles, Yahweh is translated as LORD printed in capi-tals. This name is blasphemed today, perhaps as never before, mixed with a stream of bad language, fouling the air like bad breath.

"Misusing the name of the Lord" – or "taking his name in vain" as older versions of the Bible put it – is a serious matter and increases vulnerability and sicknesses. When anyone turns to Jesus and stops blaspheming his name, they have God's smile. God loves his Son and will not hold anyone guiltless who is too free with his name.

When God covenanted with Israel, men began to do things "in the name of the Lord." Prophets could say, "I come in the name of the Lord" – with effect. False prophets placed themselves in danger. Using the actual expression "in the name of the Lord" did not matter if God was behind their work. Uttered in his name, our speech is potent.

David confronted Goliath in the name of the Lord. The giant cursed David in the name of his gods, but David replied, *"I come against you in the name of the Lord Almighty* [El Shaddai]. *This day the Lord will hand you over to me. The whole world will know that there is a God in Israel, that the Lord saves; for the battle is the Lord's and he will give all of you into our hands"* (1 Samuel 17:45-47). David was anointed and carried divine authority. With the anointing, David's stone found its mark like a bullet from a gun.

In 1 Kings 3:2 people were worshipping at shrines anywhere, pillars, altars, high places and under sacred trees all around the country *"because a temple had not yet been built for the Name of the Lord."* Nations were named as the people of their god – "the people of Baal," "the people of Ashtoreth" – but God called Israel *"my people."* The Ark of the Covenant was left overnight with the Philistine god Dagon and the image toppled over onto its face before the ark.

Devotees had to make their way to their gods as they did not move. The idea of anyone living in the presence of their god was totally unheard of. People took them offerings, left them there and went away, leaving their gods behind at the shrines, immobile. When Naaman was healed, he took with him some of the earth of Israel, thinking God was attached to the soil. But the God of Israel is not attached to any one place. He has no shrine and cannot be left behind. He said, *"Never will I leave you; never will I forsake you"* (Hebrew 13:5). The living God cannot be localized.

> The God of Israel is not attached to any one place. He has no shrine and cannot be left behind. He said, *"Never will I leave you; never will I forsake you".* The living God cannot be localized.

In Ephesus they made shrines to Diana that is Artemis. The word *"shrines"* in Acts 19:24 is actually the word "temples." Artemis was not a mobile goddess and had to have a dwelling. People said that she had fallen from heaven – as stone, and quite an ugly stone at that, according to legend. God has no earthly dwelling. Before Solomon built the Jerusalem temple, the people offered sacrifices of worship anywhere, such as at high places or groves of trees. When Solomon's temple was built they could not worship God anywhere else and yet no worshipper ever entered the central temple itself; only priests did that on behalf of worshippers. The High Priest entered its secret inner chamber once a year. There was nothing in there – no visible God. When the Roman general Titus broke into the Jerusalem temple he was baffled, finding nothing there except furniture.

When Solomon offered his prayer at the opening of the temple that he had built, he said, *"I have indeed built a magnificent temple for you, a place for you to dwell forever"* (1 Kings 8:13). However, God did not dwell there at all and Solomon knew that but he prayed on, *"Will God really dwell on earth? The heavens, even the highest heaven, cannot contain you. How much less this temple I have built! May your eyes be open toward this temple night and day"* (1 Kings 8:27-29). Time after time he asked the Lord to hear *"from heaven, your dwelling place." "This is what the Lord says: 'Heaven is my throne, and the earth is my footstool. Where is the house you will build for me? Where will my resting place be?'"* (Isaiah 66:1).

Today the truth of God's omnipresence tends to be overlooked. Certain teachings on "revivalism" suggest that God works more here or is more powerfully present there, or is exercising extra super revival power somewhere else. However logical that might seem, it is not New Testament doctrine. Certainly, great and exciting news comes from some area ever so often. Believers are naturally attracted there and why not? However, different manifestations do not mean God is more there than in other places. He is never half there or present to a degree; he is always there in his fullness, indivisible.

God is the same, unchanging at all times, but conditions change and they affect the work of God. At certain times he can break through like a volcano finding a vent. We do not know all the factors that might cause this to happen, but prayer does open up avenues for divine power. The new temple of Solomon had been completed and had waited unused for 11 months until its dedication. Then the glory of God came like a cloud and people were prostrated by his presence.

It is important to understand what the temple was for. Solomon repeatedly declared that it was for the name of the Lord (1 Kings 8:18-20). The heart of the temple was the Ark of the Covenant holding the two tables of the law. The temple was built for the Law. Solomon said, *"I have provided a place there for the ark in which is the covenant of the Lord"* (1 Kings 8:21). It was not at all a church as we know it. It was a monument, a building crystallizing or embodying God's name and a house of prayer to the name of the Lord; prayer was made **towards** the temple, not in it, except in the courtyards, where prayer was made at regular hours.

The temple declared God's name (1 Kings 8:29,44,48). There was never another building like the temple. It was there as a visible emblem of his name. Solomon prayed, *"This place of which you said, 'My Name shall be there'"* (1 Kings 8:29). Its magnificence, gold, embroideries and craftsmanship reflected the glory of God's name.

The heathen temples brought glory to the gods but God brought glory to the Jerusalem temple. The glory of heathen gods was their house or shrine but the glory of God needed no temple. He let his glory come down on Solomon's temple. Solomon built the temple to honor God, but the temple was honored by God having something to do with it.

When the Zerubbabel temple was opened after the captives returned from Babylon, and Solomon's temple had been destroyed, people thought it a very poor place. However, Haggai the prophet said, *"I will shake all nations and the desired of all nations will come and I will fill this house with my glory. The glory of this present house will be greater than the glory of the former house"* (Haggai 2:7-9). The *"desired of all nations"* was Christ himself and he came into that temple. Herod's temple (the building usually called the second temple) had been going for about a dozen years when Jesus was taken there in the arms of Mary his virgin mother.

Israel believed that with the temple they were safe. It enshrined the name of the Lord which would protect them. Standing in the temple, they supposed they were in his name and sensed that *"the name of the Lord is a strong tower; the righteous run to it and are safe"* (Proverbs 18:10). However, the temple was only a shadow of reality, a foretaste of good things to come. It was only the shadow of the Lord's wings. Everything in the temple spoke of Christ, from the carvings of the vine to the golden table of the Ark of the Covenant in the Holy of Holies. The temple represented the name of the Lord, but Christ is our temple, and we are *"in Christ."* His name is our refuge and shelter, all that his name signifies.

Jesus looked round Herod's temple. The temple was a man-made structure intended to declare his name, but Jesus himself said that he was greater than the temple (Matthew 12:6). In fact, Jesus, the Son of God, was the person whose name the temple celebrated. His name was greater than the name Herod knew for God, for God gave Christ the name above all names.

When Jesus said, *"Destroy this temple and I will raise it again in three days"* (John 2:19), people naturally thought he was talking about the temple building. In fact, he was speaking about the temple of his body (John 2:21). The temple building would indeed be destroyed; the soldiers of the Roman general Titus razed it to the ground 40 years later and even ploughed the site itself. When Jesus died on the cross, the authorities thought that they had destroyed the temple that was Jesus' body. That was not the end! Jesus had said that it would be restored three days later – and it was! Three days after Jesus' gruesome death, the true temple was raised to life. When John saw the New Jerusalem in a vision, he said, *"I did not see a temple in the city because the Lord God Almighty and the Lamb are its temple"* (Revelation 21:22).

We have a temple! When Christ rose from the dead, Herod's temple was no longer needed. Jesus was everything the temple was, and far more. No more sacrifices were needed, for he was the Lamb of God. No more showbread on the table for he was the bread of life. No more incense altar, for his name was as incense. No more ark of the covenant carrying the tables of the law, for that law was written on his heart and can be in ours (Psalm 40:8). The carving of the vine at the temple spoke of him who is the vine (see John 15:1). The refuge of the temple gives way to Christ our refuge. As Charles Wesley taught us to sing:

> *Other refuge have I none, hangs my helpless soul on Thee;*
> *Leave, ah! leave me not alone, still support and comfort me,*
> *All my trust on Thee is stayed, all my help from Thee I bring;*
> *Cover my defenseless head with the shadow of Thy wing.*

The Old Testament covenant took people as far as knowing and standing in his name, but it did not take them to the temple itself. Not one of them who was not a priest ever stood under its roof. Herod's temple had a gold roof, set with golden spikes to keep the birds from fouling the place, but it sheltered only a few favored priests. Walls were built separating Jew and Gentile, male and female, maimed and whole. When Christ became our temple, all walls were taken away. We enter without hesitation into our temple, Christ Jesus. The old covenant gave Israel God's name as a banner but the New Covenant gives us the name of Jesus. His name is not an emblem on a banner; it is written on our foreheads and we are his banner. Jesus promised that we will even be part of the temple: *"He who overcomes I will make a pillar in the temple of my God. I will also write on him my new name"* (Revelation 3:12).

God's promise is not a poetic figure of speech, but the strength to live as we pass through this world. We are in the name of Jesus. Jesus promised, *"Whoever comes to me I will in never drive away"* (John 6:37). If he does not drive us away, it means that we are in! That is why we can say "I come in the name of Jesus" or pray "in the name of Jesus", for we are in his name, in him. We declare his name, which represents everything he is, just as the temple represented him. We are the temples of God. Whatever we do, we live in his name.

We like to say "in the name of Jesus" because we are in his name, whether we specify it or not. It is not a talisman or a magic key that increases in effectiveness the more you repeat it, but we still like to repeat it over and over. It is good. Saying it is like projecting the truth as a stream of power against the false forces of evil.

We can say "in the name of the Lord" when we make a pronouncement, but it had better be in his name if we say so. Jesus warned us, *"Many will say to me on that day, 'Lord, Lord, did we not prophesy in your name, and in your name drive out demons and perform many miracles?' Then I will tell them plainly, 'I never knew you. Away from me, you evildoers!'"* (Matthew 7:22-23). The exorcists of those days were always looking for a more powerful enchantment. They observed the power of believers using the name of Jesus to cast out demons and a family of sorcerers tried using the same "technique." But they were not "in Christ." The demons did not know them and the possessed man leaped on them and gave them sound thrashing (Acts 19:13-16).

There are many divine names, but God told Moses that his name was Lord. The Old Testament Scriptures add descriptive titles to Lord. For example, *"The Lord is my shepherd,"* Yahweh Rohi (Psalm 23:1). God gave us his name to show what he truly is in himself, and he is as he was first known: "El Shaddai" – God all-sufficient. The name of the Lord is the banner of the undefeated armies of God. He is the Lord of hosts, the Lord Almighty, and in his name we have the victory.

> When Christ became our temple, all walls were taken away. We enter without hesitation into our temple, Christ Jesus.

When God sent his Son to earth, he gave instructions as to what his name would be – Jesus. *"God gave him the name that is above every name that every tongue should confess that Jesus Christ is Lord, to the glory of God the Father"* (Philippians 2:9-11). That is an extraordinary statement. We are given the secret name of God that encompasses all other names of God, everything God is. All that the names of the Lord signify for us is concentrated in the name of Jesus. *"All authority in heaven and on earth has been given to me"* (Matthew 28:18). When we are in his name, we are agents of omnipotence.

This chapter has been about the secret of power evangelism. In Christ we are linked to unlimited help. We represent him. To come in the name of Jesus is to say what Jesus would say and do what Jesus would do. We do it by proxy but also by the power of his name. How far we plunge into those depths depends on how far we know him, know his love, carry his compassion, and are ready to suffer for his love, how passionate we are for the glory of God. It means seeing our face in the mirror and recognizing his likeness.

Question

What right do we have to come "in the name of Jesus"?

CHAPTER 12

Yeast, Pearls and Fish

"Treasure hidden in a field."
Matthew 13:44

The gospel saves us from judgment and builds a bridge to heaven, but that is only the beginning. The gospel takes us into the kingdom.

Jesus told the crowds that all the prophets and the Law had prophesied and that John the Baptist was the last of the prophets (Matthew 11:11-13). Then he made the astonishing statement that the least person in the kingdom was greater than John the Baptist. This was not greatness of personality or intellect but of spiritual experience and citizenship. Kingdom people belong to a new and higher order, that of the twice-born. *"I tell you the truth; no one can see the kingdom of God unless he is born again"* (John 3:3).

The Kingdom of God fulfilled

The gospel brings the kingdom of God to fulfillment. In Matthew 13 Jesus paints several pictures of the kingdom, viewing it from different angles. If we preach the gospel, we rescue the lost from the raging sea and land them on a safe shore. That shore is the kingdom, where they are called to service. They join us as kingdom agents, personal representatives of the king. Make no mistake about it; the blood-bought children of God are tremendously special to the Father's objectives, far more than any other creature that God has made.

Christ preached the good news that the kingdom of heaven was *"at hand."* Almost all his teaching was framed in kingdom terms. After the first three Gospels, few kingdom references occur. This has been treated as a problem, but there is none. When the gospel was preached, born-again believers entered the kingdom. They do not announce its coming when it has come and they are in it; they explore it. Christ's coming was an invasion of earth by the kingdom, the D-Day of the campaign to end the devil's earthly princedom. Perhaps what Jesus said at that time needs to be understood better today.

It will answer many questions to know what the kingdom really is in Bible terms. The word "kingdom" (Greek: *basileia*) is an abstract word for "rulership" or "royalty." It is not a place, a state or territory. When Jesus said, *"My kingdom is not of this world,"* he was making it clear that he was not talking about a geographical kingdom. The kingdom is the rule of God. Jesus stated that the kingdom, the reign of God, had come with him: *"If I drive out demons by the finger of God, then the kingdom of God has come to you"* (Luke 11:20). Jesus did more than exercise kingdom power, he himself was the kingdom. In his presence foul spirits fled, the sick were healed and sins were forgiven. The kingdom is the will of the Father performed by the Son through the Holy Spirit.

> The kingdom is the will of the Father performed by the Son through the Holy Spirit. Jesus said that the kingdom of God would come *"with power"*, and on the day of Pentecost that is what actually happened. We no longer say that the kingdom is *"at hand,"* for we are now in it; we enter it when we are born again.

Jesus said that the kingdom of God would come *"with power"* (Mark 9:1), and on the day of Pentecost that is what actually happened. We no longer say that the kingdom is "at hand," for we are now in it; we enter it when we are born again (John 3:5). Christ has *"given us the kingdom"* (Luke 12:32). We are children of the kingdom. We do not create it or build it. Scripture does not say anything like that. The kingdom is unshakeable, complete, because it is the ultimate power behind all things and will extend across all heaven and earth for all eternity.

Kingdom Pictures

Matthew 13 consists of 7 parables or pictures of the kingdom. In particular, they include several references to the word of God as seed and Christ's teaching about seed-sowing. When he had finished his discourse, he asked the disciples if they understood. That is the only time that he ever checked, but he was particularly anxious that they should grasp his meaning. Obviously it is important for us, too. Jesus explains the kingdom in his typical word pictures, making his teaching that is so full of wisdom easy to grasp.

The first of those parables is the famous one about the Sower. Jesus explains it fully and thus sheds light on the other 6. The first thing we learn is that we must sow seed; there will be no harvest unless we do. Nature does not produce a harvest in any other way; the law of harvest demands sowing. The divine law is that we sow and God gives the increase. Reaping time always and only follows seedtime. Unless we preach, no one can be saved (Romans 10:14-15).

> Christ has "given us the kingdom". We do not create it or build it. Scripture does not say anything like that. The kingdom is unshakeable, complete, because it is the ultimate power behind all things and will extend across all heaven and earth for all eternity.

The Lord never does things all by himself. God does not step down and take over while we stand back and watch. That idea has no foundation in the word of God. Evangelism has been called "a work of the flesh" in contrast to events that are often called "revival." Evangelism cannot be done without "the flesh," that is, without physical effort. We must pray, but prayer alone cannot make it happen. The picture of an ideal order where everything is explained spiritually, as acts of God, is false. The Bible makes it clear in ten thousand ways that there is a work for us on earth. Revival comes when we go out, face the problems and hostility and preach the gospel, not when we do nothing other than sit at home comfortably asking God to send revival.

The Lord's Arm around the Disappointed

Jesus shows that we cannot count on precise results. Sowing the word can have varying effects, producing nothing or up to *"a hundred times what was sown"* (Matthew 13:8). Good seed does not all produce fruit, but we must sow just the same. The Lord tells us this to encourage us when our work seems to produce little. If we sow, we are not to blame ourselves or other believers if the crop is poor. We naturally worry, wondering whether something is wrong with us, or whether we are on the right track, whether God is with us, whether our motives are good, whether we have missed God's will, and so on. The answer is not in the failure of the church but in what Jesus said – reaping depends on the ground. Jesus found hard ground in Nazareth, and some whole nations seem to be Nazareths. Where there is gospel success, the people are just as ordinary as anywhere else.

Good seed does not always produce a full harvest. Jesus spoke of the effects being lost: some seeds are snatched away by birds, destroyed by the opposition; other seeds fall on shallow ground, shallow hearts; others still begin to grow but the "worries of this life" choke the new shoots like weeds. The failure has nothing to do with the seed or the sowing but rather with the circumstances; the sowing must go on regardless.

The seed of the word is always good. We do not need a new gospel or any additions to it, no modernistic genetically modified teaching. *"We have been born again, not of perishable seed, but of imperishable"* (1 Peter 1:23). The pure word carries the life-germ of the Holy Spirit. Modify the word, mix it with our own speculations and reasoning and it will fail to germinate.

Results do not depend on the sower, for anyone can sow. Both the worthy and unworthy can scatter seed. Sowers do not need to be the super-spiritual, and church leaders should never discourage or debar anyone from that work. It has surprised leaders that characters considered unfit for the task have had great victories. That would include half the characters in the Bible to begin with. We may think we are no better, either. We may feel bad about ourselves but *"the workers are few,"* said Jesus, and the work too urgent. The only qualifications needed are that we can handle seed, even if it is only a little of it.

The seed of the word should be personified in ourselves. The version of the parable in Mark's Gospel gives it a new twist: *"Others, like seed sown on good soil, hear the word, accept it, and produce a crop – thirty, sixty or even a hundred times what was sown"* (Mark 4:20). The seed sown becomes seed in ourselves, and we embody the word. Christ saves us to save others. Everyone can sow if they have something to sow. The Bible-ignorant has nothing to scatter. The word should be in us, "planted in us" (James 1:21), making us word-carriers. Gospel witnesses need to be gospel products.

The Lord puts an arm around us when we feel disappointed about our work. He points to the ground, hard as rock, or thorn bushes and weeds competing against any new growth. Some seeds fall on the path and that path is made by the sower's own feet – we are human. Whatever happens, there will be some kind of result when harvest time comes.

Here is a list of the basics of sowing and reaping as laid down by Jesus. They are very important.

1. There is no harvest without sowing.
2. The word is always good seed.
3. Sow constantly everywhere, indiscriminately.
4. There will always be a harvest.
5. In our imperfect world results will be imperfect.
6. Conditions, the ground where the seed falls,
   will affect the size of the crop.

Those basic principles do not change. So many theories have been put forward about what to do and how to do, but we should take particular notice of what Jesus said. There is no joy to compare with what we experience when we see the results of our own work. *"He who goes out weeping, carrying seed to sow, will return with songs of joy, carrying sheaves with him"* (Psalm 126:6). That is it, not filching sheaves from neighbors' barns to fill our own.

It is not easy to win people for Christ in some places. Jesus was thrust out of Nazareth, his own home town, and could work no mighty miracles there. Preachers who overlook that make demands on their congregation with challenges, calls for ever more effort, more prayer, more holiness, more sacrifice, more of this and more of that. When "revival tarries," blame is laid right, left and centre, congregations chastised and whole Christian generations castigated, but all Jesus asks is whether seed was sown, not whether the sowers were saints.

"Cast your bread upon the waters, for after many days you will find it again. Whoever watches the wind will not plant; whoever looks at the clouds will not reap" (Ecclesiastes 11:1,4). If we wait until conditions are easy, or culture, fashion, attitudes, and traditions have changed, we will never start. The early disciples went everywhere, just as Jesus instructed – *"Preach the good news to all creation"* (Mark 16:15). The Roman world was forbidding and stony, but that is where the first harvests were reaped. Jesus said we should receive wages for our work, not for our results.

Immense Profit

There is another parable about seed in Mark 4 26-29, which adds more insight into seed growth. *"This is what the kingdom of God is like. A man scatters seed on the ground. Night and day, whether he sleeps or gets up, the seed sprouts and grows, though he does not know how. All by itself the soil produces corn – first the stalk, then the ear, then the full grain in the ear."* We do not have to manufacture a harvest. *"All by itself"* is the Greek word *automatos* – easily recognizable as our word "automatically." Then comes the next stage: *"As soon as the grain is ripe, he puts the sickle to it, because the harvest has come."* That is the wonder of the gospel. Our powers of persuasion could never turn anyone to repentance and righteousness. That is the story of Israel before Christ; the prophets' eloquence and warnings turned nobody from sin. No industry of ours can manufacture kingdom results. We cannot create new birth; that is the work of the Holy Spirit.

Let's look at two more parables, the one about the pearl and the one about the treasure hidden in a field. Both tell us the same thing: a man invested everything he had to possess those treasures. Kingdom matters are not side issues. We are not offering thoughts for a quiet day, but fundamentals concerns, salvation, the redemption of a lost world, life or death, misery or joy, slavery or freedom, hell or heaven. Ultimately, everyone on earth has to face those things. For things of that magnitude, investment needs to be total. Christ's outlay was total. It signals the extreme importance of what he sought.

> The Roman world was forbidding and stony, but that is where the first harvests were reaped. Jesus said we should receive wages for our work, not for our results.

Our aims to bring in people into the kingdom matter to God and take on an eternal perspective. They represent everything for which Christ lived and died. Once gained, *"After the suffering of his soul, he will see the light of life and be satisfied"* (Isaiah 53:11). The sacrifice – the investment of time, effort and prayer – turns out to be no sacrifice at all, but immense profit.

I always find the parable of the woman making bread and using yeast exciting. Yeast grows to permeate all the bread dough. What does it mean in the Bible? There are references in Scripture to yeast as a symbol of hypocrisy and rationalism, malice and wickedness

(Matthew 16:6, 11, 1 Corinthians 5:8). However, there is nothing in the parable that suggests that meaning. Jesus said, *"The kingdom of heaven is like yeast"* (Matthew 13:33). On other occasions the Lord spoke of the leavening effect of the gospel. He told his handful of followers, *"You are the light of the world"* and *"You are the salt of the earth"* (Matthew 5:13-14).

A very real fact is that wherever the gospel is heard, it permeates and changes life. Honesty and integrity, law-abiding conduct, kindness and concern are recognized as rules of life where Christianity has spread, in contrast to hatred, revenge, "eye-for-an-eye" retaliation, anger, selfishness and indifference. Disciples leaven the whole lump, lighten the general darkness, and preserve the world from going rotten. This effect must never be overlooked. A small candle sheds light in the deepest darkness. A mere sprinkling of salt preserves large quantities of food; a small piece of yeast turns dough into palatable bread. The social effects of one conversion are always under-estimated and generally never acknowledged by the world, but the world where Christ is proclaimed is always a better world. When the law of Christ is laid aside, governments need a thousand laws to keep order. Empty churches mean full prisons. *"Blessed is the nation whose God is the Lord"* (Psalm 33:12). Every witness for Christ is a secret asset in the happiness of the world.

The parable of the mustard seed is another striking parable in Matthew 13. It said to be the smallest of seeds, growing into a sizeable tree. It is a surprise that Jesus said that, for usually the mustard plant is quite small. For it to become a tree is unnatural, although it has been known to happen. But the gospel seed is like that – it produces surprising and apparently unnatural growth. The world's ideas need pressure to be applied through advertising, publicity and hype to make any impact. By contrast, nervous Christian effort which seems to amount to nothing very much is potent seed. It produces effects although it originates in a lowly and small corner. Conversions multiply. One person turning to Christ grows into many.

I often think how one convert, even a child or teenager, can be the starting point of future decades of godliness. Young people become parents and the family puts out branches, generation after generation establishing godly dynasties. The tragedy is that the potential can be lost by backsliding. It generates a chain of unbelievers as the years go by. We do not know how far-reaching the effects will be. To serve the Lord is a positive privilege and an opportunity to do something for the future good of this needy world!

> When the law of Christ is laid aside, governments need a thousand laws to keep order. Empty churches mean full prisons.

The 7th of the parables, the Parable of the Net, concerns final things. In this imperfect world, the outcome of our labors may be mixed. A church is not a cult where everyone has to conform. It is a hospital for the sick and wounded. Jesus expected bad fish among the good. In another parable Jesus spoke of weeds among the wheat. We will never find a church where everyone is spiritually mature. Nor will there ever be one where every Christian is faithful, no leaders fail and no Christians drop out. There are plenty of Judas and Demas characters around today. The judge of all will settle matters on the Day of Judgment. No evil-hearted man or woman who has infiltrated the church will escape. We cannot judge and separate the worthy from the unworthy, the real from the unreal. Our job is sowing not weeding, casting out demons not casting out heretics. We have no mandate to set up inquisitions and courts to try one another. Our task is just to preach the word faithfully, to stand up for the truth and to bear witness to Jesus. The end is certain: the coming of the kingdom.

Questions

1. In the parable of the sower what were the essentials of success?
2. What do you think the parable of the yeast means?

The kingdom of God
is not a matter of talk but of power.

1 Corinthians 4:20

CHAPTER 13

Status

*"Do not be afraid, little flock,
for your Father has been pleased to give you the kingdom."*
Luke 12:32

A rainforest tribesman was flown straight into a modern city. He had never seen streets, buildings, motor cars, food in tins, instant fire, lights he could not blow out, automatic doors, television, or even drawings or photos. The kingdom may be brushed aside as no more than a religious figure of speech, but the kingdom of God contrasts with the world's kingdoms just as life in a rainforest contrasts with life in a big city.

To be grasped by Faith

Jesus said, *"I confer on you a kingdom, just as my Father has conferred one on me"* (Luke 22:29). The revelation of disciples "possessing" the kingdom is a new concept. It must be grasped by faith. In our present state, we have little idea of what God means, but he would not confer a triviality, a mere idea on his beloved Son, nor on us.

If we take the gospel to the world, we can claim not only that we are in the kingdom and that we are kingdom representatives, but that we have been given the kingdom. To be a kingdom man or woman means that we have left behind the rags of worldly fashions and have put on Christ. We have come into a new world, a new order. We ourselves are also new, with new thoughts, a new outlook, new attitudes and, in particular, new power. We are citizens of the kingdom. We have been naturalized, taking on the divine nature (2 Peter 1:4), which gives us full citizenship (Philippians 3:20) and the rights to all kingdom reserves. It is fundamental that we try to appreciate who and what we are in Christ and what the business of the kingdom is.

The word "kingdom" occurs 52 times in Matthew, 43 times in Luke and 20 times in Mark, but only 5 times in John, 8 times in Acts and not at all in some New Testament books. Why is that? We shall see the wonderful reason presently.

The message of Jesus was the kingdom. The aim of evangelism is to bring people into the kingdom. So let us take a look at what the kingdom is and what it is not.

A new Kind of Kingdom

First, the kingdom is not a place with material borders. Nor is it the place where we go when we die. It not about Christians taking over cities. The kingdom is *"not of this world"* as Jesus told Pontius Pilate (John 18:36). Christ in the kingdom has no armed forces. Jesus is king but did not wade through blood to sit on a throne; the only blood that was shed was his own atoning blood. His kingdom comes by prayer not warplanes. *"This, then, is how you should pray: Your kingdom come, your will be done on earth as it is in heaven"* (Matthew 6:10).

Some may think of the kingdom as "spiritual," almost make-believe, a kind of Ruritania. The kingdom is very real. Its potential is God's omnipotence. It affects more millions of people than any power on earth. It does what no government attempts or penal code can do: it salvages wasted lives, retrieves what was lost, heals, redeems, creates hope and love, repairs family break-ups, builds godly homes, and lights our faces with the dawn of a new day. Its economy is not money-based but faith-based; faith is the currency of the kingdom. No modern nation has a purpose for its existence, but the kingdom exists for the glory of God.

> To be a kingdom man or woman means that we have left behind the rags of worldly fashions and have put on Christ.

When Jesus said that his kingdom was *"not of this world,"* he was conveying a central truth to the representative of the Roman Empire, Pontius Pilate. It is a real kingdom, but of a new kind. The kingdoms of this world maintain their borders with armed forces, police and laws, but the kingdom of God does not employ anyone in such a protective or defensive role.

There have been attempts to create the kingdom on earth, such as theocracies and Christian rulership, but they have proved as much kingdoms of this world as any others. Jesus proclaimed that the kingdom had come – in its present state but not in its ultimate form. We cannot attempt to impose that and we must be clear in our thinking about that. Attempts to achieve it have been disastrous. The kingdom claims no territory and has no politics or rulers. There is no city of God on earth and we must still pray, *"Your kingdom come."* We do not know much about that future kingdom, but when Christ is King of kings, there will be a new order of things, glorious, apocalyptic and quite unimaginable.

To understand our "possession" of the kingdom, we can begin with Daniel 7:22: *"The Ancient of Days came and pronounced judgment in favor of the saints of the Most High, and the time came when they possessed the kingdom."* That Scripture has been much debated; who are the saints of the Most High and what is the kingdom; in particular, how can they possess it? Light was shed on the matter when Jesus said to the disciples, *"Do not be afraid, little flock, for your Father has been pleased to give you the kingdom"* (Luke 12:32). The *"saints"* in Daniel were the *"little flock"* that Jesus spoke of, his disciples. They would "possess the kingdom"; Jesus said that the Father had already given it to them.

Nobody is a nobody in the kingdom. We are all special. We must realize who we are and not stagger at it. We might be part of a *"little flock"* but we should lift up our heads as citizens of the eternal kingdom. Kingdom men and women are engaged hand to hand against evil and the devil. The world is a fallen and corrupt culture. Christ called us to join him and we left that dying world – we emigrated: *"He has rescued us from the dominion of darkness and brought us into the kingdom of the Son he loves"* (Colossians 1:13). We are kingdom immigrants, granted citizenship and then equipped with the armor of the Spirit.

We are God's "officials" with ownership and privileges, although to "'possess the kingdom" is not to acquire territory, a material place, anywhere on this earth. This is hard to take in but the Holy Spirit can send a shaft of light into our minds. No Bible truths are ever grasped except by faith. Exercising faith, we see the kingdom as very real, and our responsibility to it is higher than anything else demanded of us. It is the kingdom of truth. We live and act on the truth.

In its present character, the kingdom does not confer authority over people but over all the power of the enemy. We cannot pull rank on one another. All are servants of Christ, not masters. We should be *"eager to serve; not lording it over those entrusted to you. Clothe yourselves with humility toward one another"* (1 Peter 5:2-5). In Christ's kingdom there is only *"one Master and you are all brothers. You have one Father and one Teacher, the Christ. The greatest among you will be your servant"* (Matthew 23:8-11). We may impress one another by our retinue, but God does not stop at the reception or the outer office; he stands before us with a spiritual stethoscope to sound our heart.

The Children of the Kingdom

In the great Sermon on the Mount, Jesus described the character of the people of the kingdom. His first statement was: *"Blessed are the poor in spirit for theirs is the kingdom of heaven"* (Matthew 5:3). The words "is theirs" (Greek: *autoón estin*) are positive: *"the poor in Spirit"* have the kingdom. Christ went on to say, *"The meek will inherit the earth"* – a future promise. The great difference is that he did not say "the poor in spirit will inherit the kingdom" – they have it already.

Who are *"the poor in spirit"*? They were not just the poor, but the poor in spirit. In the Psalms and Proverbs, for example, the poor are referred to 75 times along with other unfortunates. Poor and rich were taken to be the natural order, with few rich people and lots of poor people. So many had nothing whatever to trust in, no money, no friends and no hope. They were the poor who turned to God as their hope. They rested their future and their troubles on him. Poverty humbled them in spirit and knocked all their crowing arrogance and self-sufficiency out of them; it left them with one option, to trust in God. The poor in spirit were people whose spirit was humble; nor longer arrogant and self-assured, they had chosen to walk with confidence in God. They possessed the kingdom. They valued the kingdom first.

The Sermon on the Mount – Matthew chapters 5 through 7 – is often misunderstood. Some call it the Christian Mount Sinai, Christ's new law. It is nothing of the kind. Jesus gave us only one law, the law of love. The Sermon on the Mount is Christ's own exposition of his law of love. His sermon described kingdom people, idealistic perhaps, but nonetheless their basic inclination and aims.

James, Jesus' brother, put it in his own words: *"Has not God chosen those who are poor in the eyes of this world to be rich in faith and to inherit the kingdom he promised those who love him?"* (James 2:5). God favors faith people, rich or poor. The poor often exercise faith because they have nothing else to fall back on. Poverty is demoralizing, crushing the heart out of people. But it can have a glorious side effect. We need not sink in a swamp of bitterness. Poverty can swing us God-ward. Grinding poverty lowers people's self-evaluation, leaving them feeling like subclass humans, nobodies who carry no weight in this world. By divine grace our leaden misfortune is transmuted into the golden experience of knowing God. It is a discipline. Poverty causes us to lean on God; life is enriched in a way that no money can achieve. God-confidence is greater than self-confidence.

The apostle Paul was poor but he said that he made many rich – by the gospel (2 Corinthians 6:10). The church is not an institution for financial gain, but as Peter said to the beggar at the temple gate, *"Silver or gold I do not have, but what I have I give you. In the name of Jesus Christ of Nazareth, walk"* (Acts 3:6). In today's affluent world how many people or churches can say, *"Silver or gold I do not have"*? On the other hand, how many can say, *"In the name of Jesus, walk?"* That is what this book is about, giving what we have, introducing people to the gospel, sharing our experience of God's love, making people well and rich in spirit, trusting in God, the children of the kingdom.

> Nobody is a nobody in the kingdom. We are all special. We must realize who we are and not stagger at it.

However, God has a place for the rich although Jesus did say, *"It is easier for a camel to go through the eye of a needle than for a rich man to enter the kingdom of God"* (Matthew 19:24). Having wealth is not a sin, but the love of wealth is fertile soil for the devil's harvest. Paul told Timothy, *"Command those who are rich in this present world not to be arrogant nor to put their hope in wealth, which is so uncertain, but to put their hope in God"* (1 Timothy 6:17). Money is like a horse meant to carry us, but we often end up carrying the horse. That is the money trap.

Not many were rich in Galilee or even in Jerusalem when Jesus visited those places. Today's world generates wealth and wealthy people. If it is hard for the rich to enter the kingdom, compared with most people at the time of Christ, we should perhaps bear in mind that we are all comparatively affluent in the third millennium, enjoying standards of which the Emperors of Rome knew nothing. It may be hard for the rich to be poor in spirit but it is not impossible. The doors of the kingdom are not slammed on the wealthy simply because of their wealth, or many of us would be out in the cold.

In fact, poverty is not God's plan. He made this planet and its vast resources, its oil, gold and forests, and put into our hands as stewards. He did not make riches for the godless nor as a test or lure for the godly. To be like God the Giver we must have something to give. He pours out goodness like an eternal sun. The purpose of evangelism is not material prosperity but through the gospel nations do prosper.

More than Theory

Jesus also said something which is like a window from which we can see the kingdom. He sent his disciples out *"to preach the kingdom of God and to heal the sick"* (Luke 9:2) – two things but the same operation. By announcing the kingdom, they healed the sick. Just as a doctor practices medicine, kingdom people impart divine healing – or kingdom power is no more than theory.

The kingdom has signs and Jesus pointed that out: *"If I drive out demons by the finger of God, then the kingdom of God has come to you"* (Luke 11:20). Sending disciples out on a mission, he said, *"When you enter a town and are welcomed, heal the sick that are there and tell them, 'The kingdom of God is near you'"* (Luke 10:8-9). Healings are evidence of the kingdom like getting wet is evidence of water.

The kingdom is more than a theological idea: *"The kingdom of God is not a matter of talk but of power"* (1 Corinthians 4:20). Jesus did not send the disciples to announce that the kingdom was coming. John the Baptist did that; Jesus began repeating John's message.

The Greek word *basileia* means "reign" and the kingdom of God is the reign of God. In his kingdom, God is not a figurehead monarch; he exercises active authority, challenging the powers of evil, the devil, darkness and disease. *"I have given you authority to overcome all the power of the enemy"* (Luke 10:19).

That is the how the kingdom is manifested at present. It is also the power exercised by Jesus. The devils were subject to him – to everyone's astonishment: *"We have seen remarkable things today,"* they said (Luke 5:26). Now, there was only ever one power, the Holy Spirit. Kingdom power is Holy Spirit power. Christ said that he cast out spirits by the finger of God and that finger is the Holy Spirit. The words *"the finger of God"* occur in only one other place in the Bible. When God was at work crushing the power of Egypt in order to release his people, Pharaoh's advisors said, *"This is the finger of God"* (Exodus 8:19). That same "finger" is what Jesus called the kingdom of God – God in action. What action! He cast out demons by the same power that overcame Egypt.

Before the gospel was preached, little was understood about the Holy Spirit. God had performed only occasional wonders in the Old Testament period. People understood what the reign of God meant but until Jesus began teaching they did not know that it involved the supernatural work of the Holy Spirit.

That is why the first three Gospels attribute all works of power to the kingdom or to the reign of God. Then the Holy Spirit of God was outpoured on the day of Pentecost. The apostles had no need to refer to it as the kingdom. They knew what it really was, namely, the Holy Spirit. We read little about the kingdom after the first three Gospels because the Holy Spirit had not yet been given, but when he was given, kingdom language became the language of the day of Pentecost.

During the 40 days when the resurrected Jesus spoke finally to the disciples, he spoke *"about the kingdom of God"* (Acts 1:3). Then he changed his terms and told them that they would be baptized with the Holy Spirit. The kingdom had operated when Jesus had the Spirit and now the disciples would have the Spirit – that is the power of the kingdom. Before the day of Pentecost they preached the kingdom of God and healed the sick by the delegated power of Christ, but after the day of Pentecost they preached Christ and healed the sick by the Holy Spirit. They "possessed the kingdom," as do all believers who minister in Holy Spirit demonstration.

Jesus had spoken of *"the night when no one can work"* (John 9:4), that is when no one could work miracles. That night began with his arrest. Until Christ had risen from the dead and ascended to the right hand of God, no miracles were seen. However, Jesus promised that they would see the kingdom come with power and that took place when the Holy Spirit was outpoured. The early disciples saw it and we see still it today.

It is so exciting! The gifts of the Holy Spirit for witnessing represent kingdom authority and resources. It is all there in the Spirit. The disciples had drawn their authority from Jesus and healed the sick during the time that he spent with them. He had delegated power to them over all the power of the enemy. Today Jesus sends the Holy Spirit, bestowed on all that call on the Father. The "poor in spirit" become mighty in God, possessors of the kingdom.

When men of God in ancient Israel preached repentance and trust in God, there was simply no response whatever. Ezekiel said they liked to hear his prophecies like a pleasant song, then went away unchanged and unaffected

> Healings
> are evidence
> of the kingdom
> like getting wet
> is evidence of water.

(Ezekiel 33:32). Why was that? Because the Holy Spirit had not been given to convict the world of sin, righteousness and judgment. But today, the simplest among us can witness and see the gospel change lives, for the Spirit has come.

That is why we are commanded, *"Be filled with the Spirit"* (Ephesians 5:18). That is the same kingdom authority that Jesus exercised, healing the sick and expelling demons. We are certainly not alone in what we do. *"You, dear children, are from God and have overcome them, because the one who is in you is greater than the one who is in the world"* (1 John 4:4). We also have allies. We are backed by the whole power of the kingdom of God. The kingdom of God is at war against the kingdom of darkness, but we are not guerrillas, each of us alone in a private war with darkness. We are part of our Captain's global strategy. He keeps in touch with us in our sector of the battle front where he needs us and has placed us.

If we are discouraged or weary, we might be tempted to feel that no one else is bothering. We might feel sorry for ourselves like Elijah the prophet. He said, *"I am the only one left."* But the Lord told him that he had 7,000 reserves that Elijah knew nothing about (1 Kings 19:15-18). The prophet Elisha knew better. When his servant came trembling with the news that they were surrounded by enemies, the prophet said, *"Don't be afraid. Those who are with us are more than those who are with them"* (2 Kings 6:16). The resources of the kingdom are supporting us.

What strength! What confidence! What a privilege!

Questions

1. What mistake did people in Jesus' time make about the kingdom of God?
2. What is our position in the kingdom?

On Target for
100,000,000 *Souls*

Evangelist Reinhard Bonnke

For over thirty years, Christ for all
Nations has been winning millions
to Christ...one soul at a time!

Jos-Nigeria

In five days of meetings, 1,276,840 people registered their decisions for Jesus Christ, and signed decision cards to that effect.

Those who have been miraculously healed during the crusade meeting share their testimonies for all in attendance to hear and rejoice!

In one meeting, 650,000 were at the Gospel Crusade in Jos…to hear AND receive the Gospel!

8,000 Fire
Conference
delegates
are inspired
to Holy Spirit
evangelism.

More than double the expected attendance
gathered for the Easter Celebration Service
at the Green Square Khartoum.

Massive
crowds
gathered,
hungry to
hear the
Gospel.
Over 210,000
people
attended six
days of
meetings.

Khartoum Sudan

UNPRECEDENTED CROWDS HEAR THE GOSPEL MESSAGE IN THE SUDANESE CAPITAL CITY

Prayer requests that are sent to the ministry from around the world are brought to the crusade to be prayed for by all in attendance.

Satanic strongholds are broken as witchcraft items and fetishes are burned!

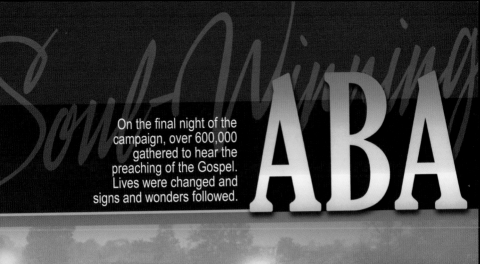

On the final night of the campaign, over 600,000 gathered to hear the preaching of the Gospel. Lives were changed and signs and wonders followed.

ABA

Soul Winning

Alongside every Gospel Campaign, CfaN holds daytime Fire Conference meetings for pastors, church leaders, and workers to be trained and equipped to reach the lost in their nation.

That same week over 1,475,000 people attended the Great Gospel Crusade held at the 'Papal Grounds' just outside the city.

The Fire Conference was held in the prestigious Eagle Square, which is surrounded by the offices of many government departments and international businesses.

Despite record-breaking attendance at the Fire Conference, all 93,000 delegates received a copy of the book *Evangelism by Fire* and were inspired to Holy Spirit evangelism.

Abuja
Fire Conference

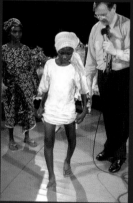

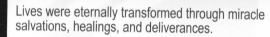

Lives were eternally transformed through miracle salvations, healings, and deliverances.

Lagos, Nigeria

3,461,171 people made a decision for Christ in the six days of meetings!
Over 1,600,000 people assembled for the final night of the campaign.

Up to 600,000 people attended a single service of the Great Gospel Crusade. During the week, a total of 1,600,000 gathered at the grounds of the University of Calabar for the evening meetings.

When the Gospel net was cast in the fishing community of Calabar, an abundant harvest of souls was won for the Lord!

Calabar
Nigeria

In many African cities, Reinhard Bonnke is welcomed as an honored guest at the Royal Palace. The King of Calabar told Evangelist Bonnke, "I hereby give you the kingdom of Calabar...to do the will of God."

Each and every person who makes a decision for Christ is counseled and connected to a local church.

At the Port Harcourt Gospel Crusade, literally hundreds of people pushed toward the side of the platform each evening to testify of their miraculous healing. The blind saw, the deaf heard, and the cripples walked.

The campaign, in the "Sandfill Area," was attended by more than 2,100,000 people in the five nights of meetings.

PORT HARCOURT
Nigeria

Literature Seeding

Now that You are Saved booklets, shipped to campaign sites in 20-foot containers, are given to every new believer. These small booklets form the vital link between each convert and the local church follow-up program.

As part of the ministry's discipleship-training program, over 178 million copies of CfaN books and booklets have been published in 140 languages and printed in 53 countries. Millions of books have been freely 'seeded' throughout the world.

CfaN CHRIST FOR ALL NATIONS

CHAPTER 14

Good Health!

"Heal the sick, cleanse those who have leprosy."
Matthew 10:8

Half a billion Christians experience salvation for body and soul today. The Holy Spirit is testifying to the whole world that the Lord is the God of heaven and earth and has all power in heaven and on earth. Healings, wonders and deliverances multiplying to the point of becoming commonplace make God evident everywhere and the controversy about whether God still does these things is long past.

Nevertheless, our faith must rest in the word of God. Experience is not a second Bible. The word is God-science; believe it because the word says it. Without the word we may be hopeful. With the word we have faith.

We have been told not to testify of healings because it could build up false hopes and create disillusionment. In that case we had better close our Bibles for ever. The word is the source of all expectation, the greatest encourager of hope. The fact is that the faith of people coming forward for prayer is usually hardly a glimmer, often so weak that it binds the hand of God. We can expect opposition to the healing ministry. It was the experience of Jesus in Nazareth, where he could do very little and the people wanted to kill him. That is the truth about human nature – it is perverse.

Many claim to build on the Scriptures but they amaze us with their clashing architectural differences, especially on certain subjects. The reason is that they are pirouetting on a small area of Scripture. In contrast, the truth of divine healing is blazoned right through the Old and New Testaments as a mark of the character and habitual behavior of God. Healing has abundant backing in the word.

To preach the word implies faith in God's healing mercies, part of our gospel to *"all creation"* (Mark 16:15). God is concerned with human well-being, safety, health, and freedom, the blessings on earth of righteousness. *"Jesus Christ has brought life and immortality to light through the gospel"* (2 Timothy 1:18).

Jesus radiated God: *"The Son is the radiance of God's glory and the exact representation of his being"* (Hebrew 1:3). He was God in the flesh – not on and off, not in phases, but all the time. He spent far more time healing the sick than talking about heaven and in doing so he represented what God is. We say that actions speak louder than words. In God, we have both; God declares what he is by his acts and they correspond to his word. By healing he declares himself the Lord who heals. Jesus healed the sick because God is like that.

> Our faith must rest in the word of God. Experience is not a second Bible. The word is God-science; believe it because the word says it. Without the word we may be hopeful. With the word we have faith.

A huge segment of the world church has assumed for centuries that God is only interested in religion, or in spiritual and heavenly affairs. But God's promises are to living people, not to the spirits of the dead. We are not ghosts; he loves people. We were created to move in the spiritual dimension but we were made from the dust of the ground. Our destiny is not as pure spirits in heaven, but to be like Jesus in his resurrection.

God vested his interests here in this planet and sent his Son whose body was made of the clay of this planet like ours. He sent him to be part of this visible, touchable world. We are God's creatures and our instinct is not wrong when we take it for granted that God should take care of us. Naturally, when things go wrong we ask, "Why did God allow that?" However, that is not the same as discounting what is so obviously part of Scripture.

Some (called deists) speak of God making the world and then retiring, letting the world go on as it may. Pantheists cannot perceive the divine dimension but speak of God as part of the world itself. It is all so crude. It is gloriously wonderful that our Creator became a creature in creation to save human creatures. All Christ's dealings have been with our physical world and our physical needs. Healing is the window display of the kingdom of God.

Thinkers have arrogantly assumed their thought is superior to the revelation of God and have spent 300 years trying to write the life of Christ without miracles. That is impossible. The only Jesus we know predominantly worked miracles. Take that away and Jesus becomes a legend, a shadow, and a figure that could never have made the impact on the world which he has. A Jesus who no longer healed could never be the Jesus who is *"the same yesterday and today and for ever"* (Hebrew 13:8).

Healing gives meaning and reality to God's attributes of omniscience, omnipotence and omnipresence and to his love, mercy, forgiveness, goodness, agelessness, and faithfulness. The Creator would never be happy doing nothing in his creation any more than a human gardener puts plants in his garden and never touches it again. Healing lifts doctrines out of the theological text books into the realm of warm and common experience.

Truth is treated today as something to think about, but in Scripture it is something to experience. God never provided academic "truth" as a topic for scholarly debate. Many are too intellectually proud to admit their need of a living Savior. The truth is Jesus – not an equation, not a statement, but a person stretching out a hand to the broken and the sick, out in the streets loving and healing the common people.

In the healing ministry we have to take human perversity into account. God does not submit to tests. If we do not believe, it is our loss, not God's loss. King Herod had Jesus brought into his palace and thought that Jesus would assert himself with a miracle or two. Jesus had no time for that man, whom he called a *"fox"* (Luke 13:32).

Is the world willing to let Jesus be what he is and do what he would like to do? All too often people do not want evidence. They ask for it as a disguise and cover for their unbelief. On one occasion Jesus was in a synagogue where there was a man with a shriveled hand (Mark 3:1-6). We read that *"some of them were looking for a reason to accuse Jesus, so they watched him closely to see if he would heal him on the Sabbath."* Those people made evil of Christ's good. They were his enemies because of his divine power. At the same time, they were sure that Jesus would heal the man; Christ's enemies then had more faith than some modern Christians. Villains in the synagogue knew that healing was typical of Jesus, but in many churches today people do not know that.

Human Nature

John 5 contains another revelation about human nature. The pool at Bethesda was regarded as having healing properties. It was believed that when the water bubbled, the first person to slip into the water would be cured. One unfortunate always missed his chance; someone got there before him. Jesus came and asked him a question that seems very odd in the circumstances, *"Do you want to get well?"* (v 6). Would he be in Bethesda at all if he did not want to get well? Jesus knew human nature that not every sick person really wants to get well. Modern doctors know that there are many motives behind continuing sickness, and church healing sessions find that some people who come forward for healing with an apparent desire to be well are inwardly anxious about the total life change that healing would mean. For some it would prove God to them, and that too would make demands on them to live a godly life.

At Bethesda the man did not answer Jesus, "Yes, I do want to get well!" but began making excuses for still being sick. Jesus cut short his talk and said, *"Get up! Pick your up mat and walk"* (v 8). He did.

In all dealings with God, human nature proves an uncertain factor. Healings do not take place sometimes because people are not mentally geared for it and often not spiritually ready. The same applies to salvation. Christ is asking everyone if they wish to be made whole, saved, but excuses sprout like dandelions in spring. Often people take it as a cue to argue about religion, although they need the help, peace and direction in life that Christ has for them.

They even look elsewhere like the sick man at Bethesda and excuse themselves saying, "Well, I did search!" Yes, but they stayed sick or unsaved. They searched when they could have found. People are lost and try to find their own way, too self-proud to accept they cannot manage on their own and that they need Jesus.

> We minister for compassion's sake. Some seek healing powers because they want power and want to be known. Laying on hands is a mark of love, gentleness, and concern. It is an empty gesture if the wish behind it is to impress or be admired as a person of power. To God be all the glory for ever.

The sick man at Bethesda was healed by doing exactly what Jesus said. He carried his rolled up bed conspicuously on his shoulder in Jerusalem on the Sabbath day. That shocked the strictly religious. People strongly objected to Jesus telling the man to do that. They did not approve of that kind of Jesus. The real Jesus still shocks! The scholars looking for the historic Christ discredit the stories of his healing wonders – they do not want that kind of Jesus. It does not fit their scholastic attitude.

Only an odd healing or two are recorded before Jesus came to earth, but when people were sick and got well again, they gave praise to God: *"Praise the Lord, O my soul; all my inmost being, praise his holy name – who forgives all your sins, and heals all your diseases"* (Psalm 103:1-3). In Israel they believed that God – and only God – healed. To be sick meant that God was grieved with them, and to get well meant that he had forgiven them. This is a spiritual basis. Sin brought sickness into the world. When God heals, the consequence of human failure is lifted.

"By his wounds we are healed" (Isaiah 53:5). Without the work of Christ, healing would be impossible. Matthew (8:17) quotes Isaiah: *"He took up our infirmities and carried our diseases."* The reality of Christ's dealing with sin is that healings take place. The cross is the sure ground. If Jesus died for me, what would he not do for me? *"He who did not spare his own Son, but gave him up for us all – how will he not also give us all things?"* (Romans 8:32).

Healing comes from the Heart of God

Healing proves that long ago the work was done, by the mighty act of God in Christ. To give us his Son was greater than making the stars. It was the greatest act of a God who performs the impossible. To suggest that he could not or would not heal a sickness is ludicrous. A mountain in labor does not bring forth a mouse, and mount Calvary did not bring forth a minor effect; God's labor produces more than words, a text book doctrine; it produces power, hope, forgiveness, and healing.

If anyone wants to study healing in the Scriptures, they will need to study every verse. They need to search out the character, disposition, and nature of God. Healing does not arise from a plan made by God but from his heart. He heals because that is his nature.

Problems have been created by theories gratuitously imported into Scripture: "God may be teaching me a lesson"; "It may not be God's will"; "It may not be God's time"; "Miracles were only for the apostolic age"; "I'm not a faith person." We could go on recounting excuses for unbelief. The commonest feeling is that healing or other physical blessings need very rare and powerful faith. That is a fallacy. The only faith we need is simply to know the word and accept it, to be locked on to the word.

When healing is delayed, it must not be assumed that faith has failed. Faith never fails. We leave the issue to God. Healing is his work, for his glory, and he is well able to look after himself – and after us.

We minister for compassion's sake. Some seek healing powers because they want power and want to be known. Laying on hands is a mark of love, gentleness, and concern. It is an empty gesture if the wish behind it is to impress or be admired as a person of power. To God be all the glory for ever.

Question

What role does healing play in spreading the gospel?

There are different kinds of gifts, but the same Spirit.
There are different kinds of service, but the same Lord.
There are different kinds of working,
but the same God works all of them in all men.
Now to each one the manifestation of the
Spirit is given for the common good.

1 Corinthians 12:4-7

CHAPTER 15

Gifted

*"To each one the manifestation of the Spirit
is given for the common good."*

1 Corinthians 12:7

The great men of the Bible were all charismatics. There was no leadership except by Spirit-endowed men and women. From Moses right through the Old Testament, Joshua, all the Judges, David, and to the prophets, *"men spoke from God as they were carried along by the Holy Spirit"* (2 Peter 1:21). Saul, the first king of Israel, was anointed to qualify him for his position. After the prophet Malachi, Christ came and told the disciples not to start their witness until they were endued with power from on high. That is the only way that people were supposed to work for God, by his anointing. Not even Jesus ministered until the Spirit rested on him in Jordan. The first promise of John the Baptist about Jesus is that he would baptize his followers in the Holy Spirit.

That is the whole scenario, God breaking in on mankind. He does not leave us to get on with it while he waits in the wings. That is a totally false conception and totally contrary to the whole word of God. The Holy Spirit is not an optional extra that is given us if we concentrate and pray. It is what Christianity is all about – the union of man with God through the Spirit. Jesus himself was the transcendent role model. He said, *"Ask and you will receive"* – meaning the Holy Spirit.

This vital theme echoes again and again through the Scriptures. Until Pentecost, nothing was understood about the "gifts" of the Spirit. Certain manifestations, such as speaking in tongues and healing, became regular and were accepted as the norm. People knew that the new converts had been given the Spirit *"for they heard them speaking in tongues"* (Acts 10:46). That was the sign gift. No other sign is ever mentioned and it is understood when not mentioned.

Gifts for the Ungifted

Paul analyzed these manifestations and classified them in his lists. He is the only one of the New Testament writers to help us to sort out our experiences in these things. The modern Pentecostal/ Charismatic movement has developed understanding of the activities of the Spirit from his teaching in 1 Corinthians. Nonetheless, the Spirit may overstep our definitions for God is always greater than our theology.

Paul wrote that we ought not to be ignorant of spiritual gifts. However, ignorance has been prevalent through the centuries. Theology and Bible commentaries have treated the subject as one of mystery, things that happened once that we do not understand now. We should understand – especially to avoid mistakes, misuse and abuse of charismatic endowments.

Let us look closely at that important passage in 1 Corinthians 12:

"There are different kinds of gifts, but the same Spirit. There are different kinds of service, but the same Lord. There are different kinds of working, but the same God works all of them in all men. Now to each one the manifestation of the Spirit is given for the common good." (1 Corinthians 12:4-7)

The Holy Spirit takes anyone up. He does not choose as we choose. He does not need to do so. He can make anything of anybody, just as he likes. Obviously, speaking in tongues is not just for linguists. It is of God so anyone can be endowed. I myself was 11 years old when Acts chapter two was repeated for me personally. The gift of the word of wisdom or knowledge is not exclusively for the wise and learned. His gifts are for the ungifted, for **all** who believe.

The history of God's choice of men is astounding. Luther was an unknown monk, Wesley a failed missionary, Charles Finney – who won a million Americans for Christ – was a small-town lawyer, Dwight L. Moody – who shook London – was a shoe salesman. In England, the greatest evangelist since Wesley, George Jeffreys, was a grocers' assistant, and Billy Graham was only a Youth for Christ staff evangelist when he began. I myself could claim to be nothing at all, just an evangelist.

The secular, philistine world focuses on its own great ones, the stars of stage, sport and politics. It does not know what is really going on under its proud nose. If they hear news of the Holy Spirit, salvation, healing, blessing and righteousness, they are uncomprehending. Any chance references by the media leave them dumb and bemused, but generally the very existence of the Christian world is ignored. A murder fills yards of newspaper columns but the news of, say, a million turning to Christ, as in a CfaN campaign, is met with stony silence. The public is cheated of the truth, misinformed and even brainwashed.

> The Holy Spirit takes anyone up. He does not choose as we choose. He does not need to do so. He can make anything of anybody, just as he likes. His gifts are for the ungifted, for **all** who believe.

Paul spoke of himself as *"known, yet regarded as unknown"* (2 Corinthians 6:9). The godless are like the people on the walls of Jericho gazing down bemused as Israel's tribes walked round and round the town every day for a week, an unmilitary-looking rabble. On the last day they discovered that with God those robed priests were earth-shaking. For that matter, it was the same over Jesus. They crucified him and went home to tea. Today he strides the continents, the world's greatest contemporary. Far more people turn to him and are "born again" every day than are born, but his name is rarely mentioned outside Christian enclaves.

What God does has to do with what we do

Whatever the Holy Spirit does is not for mere intellectual or popular interest or even to give us a pleasurable experience; it has a practical outcome. He gives gifts for useful purpose, not for our pride of possession or to impress everybody. How many want "the gift of healing" as a mark of their own distinction? God gives gifts to those who give themselves to him. They are his, for him, the means of his purposes and are intended to be *"for the common good."*

The gifts are God's gifts and he operates them himself: *"to each one the manifestation of the Spirit is given."* God rarely gives anything outright for independent use. He usually keeps his hand in affairs. Eternal life is a constant inflow, and so is the gift of the Spirit. Each operation of a gift is under his control as a manifestation of his will, as we read, that the Spirit *"gives them to each one, just as he determines"* (1 Corinthians 12:11).

For example, *"to one there is given through the Spirit the message of wisdom"* (1 Corinthians 12:8). Note that it is not a residential ability but a particular word as the Spirit gives it, as a manifestation. No gifts reside in us making us independent, operating as we desire, but only as he determines and as the Spirit flows through us.

Each person is an organ or channel for him. He does not work haphazardly, flitting from one to another without a clear purpose. He not only gives gifts but the same Spirit gives ministries, "operations," or callings. The gift of tongues is a ministry. Just as everyone can speak but some are called to preach, so by the Spirit we may all speak in tongues, but God takes up some for a specific purpose in the church. It becomes their ministry.

Everyone can lay hands on the sick, but for some it is a special "operation" or ministry. We are told to use our gifts (Romans 12:6-8), that is, to recognize them and live prepared for that service. The same applies to all gifts. God chooses one person or another as his usual instrument for a particular gift.

Service gifts produce unity. "Gifts" are listed in the first 11 verses of 1 Corinthians 12. The whole passage concerns unity, as does the whole epistle, in fact. Paul wrote because he had heard of disunity in the church. Paul pictures the gifts creating unity. This is unity in diversity, many gifts, operations, and services moved by one Spirit. This unity is not intended to make us all a solid block of identical molecules; each person is unique, like parts of a physical body – head, feet, eyes, and so on. We know far more about the body now and that DNA cells have profuse differences. The greatest differences in creation are between one human being and another. We have whole dimensions of varied personality traits unknown to other creatures, and it takes all sorts to make a church. The church is the greatest of all God's creations, the greatest thing on earth or in heaven, produced by infinite wisdom and Christ's suffering. Just as Eve was taken from the side of Adam, the church was formed from the wounded side of Jesus, the second Adam. The gifts of the Spirit are not everything, but they do constitute part of that amazing new creation, the church. No writer has ever imagined such a glorious entity, one with God, and one with one another bound together by a common life force.

The Holy Spirit alone creates this unique oneness. It is not the product of good organization. It means more than agreeing with one another or getting together. It is a wonderful complexity that God had planned from eternity for future eternities. The church is the greatest of all wonders and in the end will be seen as the only thing that matters. Whether or not the world relates to the church is irrelevant: *"The world and its desires pass away but the man who does the will of God lives for ever"* (1 John 2:17).

The order of God does not hinder human organization. God is not the God of disorder but of order. He does not want a ramshackle, anything-goes church on earth. However, he does not specify for us a particular form of order or organization, providing we *"keep the unity of the Spirit through the bond of peace"* (Ephesians 4:3). His unity is not uniformity. However, attitudes can fissure the unity of the Spirit like cracks in the rock. If one organization is at loggerheads with another, it destroys the unity of the Spirit. How can the Holy Spirit rest in and bless a church that is falling out with another church? We are not responsible for creating unity – only God has that power, but what we cannot create we can keep, all working for the same faith to the same end. The word "keep" is used 75 times in the New Testament. God does things, and we must keep them much as God created a garden and set Adam in it to keep it. Churches either belong to a denomination or are a denomination on their own. If one denomination of believers sets against another, it disgraces God and his work on earth, the church.

That is the true basis of the Holy Spirit gifts. All gifted people depend on one another. Nobody has all the gifts and not all have the same gifts. Each kind of working, gift and ministry complete the body of Christ, the church, by the Spirit, that God may be all in all. Just as our feet need our head and our hands need our eyes, we all need one another, whether we realize it or not. That is the unseen unity of the body. No church is just for tongues speakers or for expellers of demons. A gift is exercised on behalf of the whole church, especially the church where we are.

If I lay hands on the sick, they are the hands of the body of Christ – in a sense everybody's hands. I am not a pair of hands moving without a body, but my hands or my voice are one with every believer present. In the New Testament, the church is always the local church. So the gifts unite the local church, for they are all by one Spirit and that is the Spirit of unity.

All gifts are given by grace. Paul coins his words for gifts though no parts of the words include the word "gift." What God gives is manifestations rather than outright abilities or powers. On the whole he avoids the concept of gifts. The word in the original Greek text is *pneumatikon*. The closest translation is "spiritualities."

All gifts are grace gifts but not all grace gifts are miracle gifts. There are many grace gifts that are not miracle gifts. The Corinthians loved the gifts which displayed power, but Paul stressed other gifts of character. Paul told the Roman church that he would go there to impart *"some spiritual gift to make you strong"* (Romans 1:11). The gift was for the whole church, not for an individual. He himself said that miracle gifts were given by the choice of God, not of man. Nonetheless, through his ministry in Rome he would add a gift of grace to the whole body.

The gifts operate *"for the common good,"* that is, when Christians meet together in fellowship. The miracle-working Spirit also operates outside the fellowship, but in 1 Corinthians Paul is talking about gifts within the church. The "gift of tongues" was a manifestation of the Spirit in the fellowship of believers. The gift of *"gifts of healings"* (1 Corinthians 12:28) was especially for believers in fellowship, but God operates in the same way to needy sick folk outside in the world. Jesus touched and healed people of all kinds and from different areas without asking what they believed or what their religion was (Matthew 4:23-25). He is our example and mentor. The apostles also operated on the same principle. John and Peter healed a cripple saying, *"What we have we give you"* (Acts 3:6) – that is, a gift of his healing. Scripture says that God is good to all.

The Essence of Christian Witness

Jesus told the disciples to wait for the Holy Spirit and that he would make them witnesses, witnesses to him, his personal representatives. They could not be "witnesses" to a doctrine. They would represent him when he gave them the Holy Spirit and his power. Doing his works would identify them with him. This was not merely the power of persuasion but the power of Christ, the origin and source of all power. He was *"declared with power to be the Son of God"* (Romans 1:4), and his church should be declared his church by the same evidence and token.

Evangelism and witness for Christ is not intended to be a lone struggle. The essence of Christian witness is the Holy Spirit. It is the power of the Spirit breaking into the world through and for the word of God, as promised in Joel 2:28. There is no Christianity without the Spirit and no Spirit without the word. It is not just a doctrine, not just power, but always the word and Spirit through us. The accompanying signs that confirm the gospel are clearly stated in Mark 16: casting out evil spirits, speaking in tongues, healing, and divine protection against serpents and poison.

Christian "evidences," polemics, arguments, and science may be part of the work of the church, but the actual evidence is that what we preach about Christ is repeated today. We are not so much proving what happened as demonstrating that it does happen now. Jesus does what he did. Bible days have never ended. Through the Spirit in the church he still works as he determines.

The gifts of the Spirit are there for our work of witness but, as I explained above, not all of them are miracle gifts. The greatest gift, or the greatest "working," is that strange evangelistic gifting that touches the hearts of unconverted listeners and brings them repentance and faith. Pre-eminently, God's work is salvation, and his power is particularly intended to bring about that great purpose. Men and women who have led multitudes to Christ have not achieved it by great intellectual endowment but by lives filled with the Spirit and with hearts of passionate concern.

As the Spirit wills

There are 9 miracle gifts listed by Paul in 1 Corinthians 12. Paul's letters contain many lists and they are not exhaustive but general. The Holy Spirit may work in other fashions besides the 9 gifts listed by Paul. All the miracle gifts operate as the Holy Spirit wills, not just at the will of witnesses and preachers. Nevertheless, God honors his servants' boldness when they step out in faith like Elijah on Mount Carmel. Note the word of caution, for arrogance is not a substitute for genuine faith which is a gift of the Spirit. Boldly telling someone "You are healed" may not be faith but presumption. Let the patient testify first.

Paul lists the word of knowledge and the word of wisdom. He is not talking about knowledge and wisdom in general, but a specific "word" for a specific circumstance. The Spirit gives it *"as he determines."* Nonetheless, as witnesses we must remain open for what the Spirit wants to do and not hold back in fear when he speaks to us. He will never fail us. That is a powerful factor when we face unbelievers, if we humbly obey the promptings of God.

Healing powers and the ability to cast out unclean spirits are an inherent part of the gospel proclamation. The gift of healing is resident in the church. *"These signs will accompany those who believe: In my name they will drive out demons; they will place their hands on sick people and they will get well"* (Mark 16:17-18). Anyone can lay hands on sick people for their recovery, and it can be part – a tactful part – of personal witnessing

This short chapter had to be included in this book on evangelism, for without the gifts of the Spirit we go into battle with less equipment that we should. For a fuller explanation, see my book "Mighty Manifestations". In our campaigns we have relied totally upon the workings of the Holy Spirit and been ready for any word or gift from him at any time.

Earnestly seek the gifts of God.

Question

On what basis should the gifts of the Spirit operate?

And the scripture was fulfilled that says,
Abraham believed God,
and it was credited to him as righteousness,
and he was called God's friend.

James 2:23

CHAPTER 16

El Olam

"He cannot disown himself."
2 Timothy 2:13

We know where we are with God. He does not expect us to grasp his divine expertise at the keyboard of power and providence, but we know that he makes no mistakes and is not experimenting. A friend told me that he spoke not so long ago on the subject of "Things God cannot do." Someone objected that nothing is too hard for God but my friend quoted *"God cannot disown himself"* (2 Timothy 2:13). He cannot act against his own nature and do things that are contrary to the person that he has revealed to us.

God's unvarying Nature

Genesis 21:22-34 is an inspired story, often overlooked, about God's unvarying nature. Abraham, the father of all believers, had a lively encounter with Abimelech, a Philistine chief, possibly from Crete, who was attempting to settle in the area. No doubt Abimelech had brought his armed supporters, but so had Abraham, for grazing land and water were the vital issues. As the story is recounted in Genesis, Abimelech made wordy protestations of innocence – too wordy to be convincing and Abraham did not trust him too much. However, he and Abimelech came to an agreement and swore an oath of mutual trust to allow each another space, in particular acknowledging that an important well belonged to Abraham. In days with no government or official land registration, or even written documentation, only an oath of that kind carried any guarantee – and then only as much as a man's word was his bond.

To make the moment memorable and as a sign of goodwill and guarantee, Abraham gave Abimelech gifts from his flocks and herds. Abimelech does not appear to have given Abraham anything. To make the covenant even more positive, the well was called Beersheba, "the well of the oath."

Unsure of Abimelech and to further strengthen his rights, Abraham gave Abimelech an extra gift of 7 female lambs. When the Philistine chief went away, Abraham planted a tamarisk tree as a sign of his covenanted ownership of the well. Tamarisks are hardy trees well suited to dry wilderness conditions, an apt symbol of enduring fidelity.

Abraham was unsure about Abimelech but sure of God. At the well he *"called upon the name of the Lord"* (Genesis 21:33). He did not know God by the name Yahweh, the name that was revealed to Moses (Exodus 6:3). But he knew God and called him El Olam, God eternal. God had already begun revealing himself to Abraham as his friend (James 2:23). The patriarch knew that the Most High God could not be like the pagan deities, shifty and untrustworthy; the Most High was faithful. If we are to turn others back to God, this Scripture is encouraging. We must rely on the promise and faithfulness of God.

To Abraham God was El Elyon, the Most High God, but he realized that he was also El Olam, the eternal God. Further revelation came later in the tremendous drama of Jacob, Abraham's grandson. Slowly he had experimented with a relationship with God, the God of Abraham and the God of his father Isaac, but had not made him his own God. Then Jacob had an encounter with a "man" who wrestled with him all through the night. As day dawned the "man" gave Jacob the new name of Israel. That name includes El, meaning God. Israel built an altar to God, El Elohe Israel, meaning "God is the God of Israel". In that phrase God is named three times. At last the world would hear about the God of Abraham, Isaac and Jacob – not Israel for God is *"numbered with the transgressors,"* as Isaiah said (Isaiah 53:12).

For 20 years Jacob had traded on the fact that God was his father's and grandfather's God. He bargained with God, promising him that if he did this and that, he would accept him as his God (Genesis 28:20). God patiently ignored this patronizing and condescending arrogance. His endless grace reached out to Jacob to bring him into fellowship with himself. It is amazing that he let himself be known as the God of Jacob, the name of a crooked man. The world had known nothing about the living God and now, centuries later, he would be only Jacob's God, the God of a sinner. Identifying with Jacob conferred no honor on God. But that is God – the friend of sinners, so gracious and so understanding. We dare to call ourselves after the name of Christ – Christians. He accepts us and trusts us to represent him. What the world thinks of Christ comes only from Christians and what they are like.

The book of Genesis begins the story of God, of what he is. It assures us of his eternal goodness, character and purpose. Our faithfulness consists of trust in God's faithfulness. Faithful witnesses should be full of faith, alight with conviction. If we preach "Believe in the Lord Jesus Christ," we need to be lively believers ourselves, not "make-believers."

God does not anoint "honest doubts"

God was first distinguished by one positive mark: he was the God of faithfulness. No other god ever was. The gods of pagan myths were always represented as unpredictable, with all the same failings as earthlings. In the Greek stories creation was the result of war and murder among the gods.

The opening lines of Genesis, describing creation, are great leaps into glorious reality, like the sun rising over a vast landscape. The Genesis chapters go on to show a living God in a class of his own, far beyond all gods of human invention. No deity could be his equal. The Bible God is gracious, merciful and longsuffering, longing to bless the whole world. That is his basic nature.

> Ordinary bushes, like ordinary preaching, excite no interest – unless they are on fire.

The Bible constantly testifies to it and has been a light through a thousand years of dark ignorance.

Unbelief suggests that what God was and did in the past is not paralleled by what he is and does today. What kind of God is that? Unfortunately, it is the God of many Bible-teaching circles. They have run up against the rock, the absolute changeless character of God in all his dealings with us. The God of Bible people is our God today, or we may as well close our Bibles. Of course, not opening their Bibles is another great mistake that people make!

Witnesses somehow gravitate to where people will respond and be saved. God sees to that. It is the law of faith. If we have a sickle in our hands, God will lead us to a harvest field. He does not hand out sickles to people with no field to reap.

Without faith it is impossible to please God. He does not anoint "honest doubts." What is there to anoint? A doubting witness is no witness at all. Faith is not a process of logic. God does not fit our syllogisms.

Faith shows. So does doubt. Body language speaks as loud as any sermon. Without faith a man has neither light nor movement, like an unlit lamppost firmly concreted in. Moses turned aside to see an ordinary bush only when it was on fire. Ordinary bushes, like ordinary preaching, excite no interest – unless they are on fire.

Faith is the door to a positive life. Here is a graphic example. Imagine, if you can, a husband coming home beaming with joy, hugging his wife and children with excitement, saying, "Wonderful – I have become an unbeliever! It's made me feel so good, so full of life, I want to love everybody. I'll be a better husband and father, no drink, no gambling, no bad temper! I'm an atheist, and I'm cured!"

Utter nonsense, of course. That man's wife would never go around saying, "My husband has stopped believing in God and he's so lovely now, a brand new man." That kind of change does not happen. Men do come home full of happiness, changed and loving, but only through faith in God. It is a frequent miracle. It is *an inexpressible and glorious joy,*" said Peter (1 Peter 1:8). To produce that joy through our witness is an unparalleled privilege.

If we can speak of God having a problem, it is that of leading us into faith. From the very beginning, by one means and another, he has condescended to assure us of his faithfulness. For example, men have always made covenants. In early times those covenants took the form of oaths, with a hand being placed under the thigh of the person to whom the oath was sworn, and of blood bonds; nowadays they are in the form of legal contracts and affidavits as guarantees. The legal document in the conveyance of a house today carries red seals, recalling the time when guarantees were given with blood. God has condescended to "sign" the same kind of guarantee in order to give us assurance. Scripture describes him as the covenant God.

In Genesis 9:12-17 God covenanted with, or rather for, creation, a unilateral and unconditional declaration of intent, with promises made to the animals, birds and fish and to all mankind for ever. God promises to keep faithful even to ducks and whales. Three chapters later (Genesis 12) he made his first personal promise – to Abraham – and sooner after confirmed it by a covenant made with blood. This was not to remind himself of an obligation, for it would be impossible for him to fail, but for Abraham's sake, to give him confidence. After all, Abraham hardly knew God at the time, except as *"the Most High God,"* the greatest among gods. In Genesis 15:8-21 Abraham did as God told him, presenting animals which he had killed, dividing them in two and laying them on the ground. Then Abraham saw God move between the pieces on the ground like a blazing torch, again stating his promises to Abraham. God kept his word and four centuries later, when Abraham's descendents had become a nation, God made a covenant with them. Moses splashed blood on the people and said, *"This is the blood of the covenant that the Lord has made with you"* (Exodus 24:8).

Blood covenants are, however, mere shadows of reality. The day came when Jesus said, *"This cup is the new covenant in my blood"* (Luke 22:20). His word signified absolute faithfulness. Our soul's destiny hangs upon it. We need have no fear. His blood seals our eternity.

> *He by himself hath sworn, I on his oath depend;*
> *I shall, on angels' wings upborne, to heav'n ascend;*
> *I shall behold his face, I shall his power adore*
> *And sing the wonders of his grace for evermore.*
>
> Thomas Olivers, ca. 1770

The foundation of the whole universe is God's changelessness. Nature itself, even the changes, is not chaotic. Belief in the God of order shaped the mind of Western nations with the firm assumption that creation itself is orderly and regulated by unchanging laws. This made science possible. It could not have risen anywhere except where belief in a God of order and faithfulness prevailed. The 21st century has been infected by irreligion, loss of the knowledge of the God of faithfulness, which is undermining trust even in the physical sciences.

The God of Abraham is faithful – it has been proved over 4,000 years. To trust somebody we do not know is credulity and superstition, not faith. But our faith registers because as John wrote, *"We know him who is true"* (1 John 5:20). Faith is essentially for the future. However worthy someone may have been in the past, we have to trust them for the future – even in the case of God. God has done great things, and they are the sign and prophecy of what he is now and what he will do in the future. For the days ahead, no matter what, having faith means to vest our lives in what he will be.

I have seen God moving in power, salvation and healing, and baptizing in the Spirit. Those things are past occurrences but I know the God whose very name is *"Faithful and True"* (Revelation 19:11). I know that he does not change. Today and tomorrow he will bless us in the same way.

To preach and witness to the gospel is the greatest thing we can ever do for anybody. The gospel must be believed and our job is to preach it so it can be believed. True faith is never disappointed. What follows is some positive teaching on this matter.

Descriptions of Faith

The whole Bible is written to set our faith alight. The Bible is the faith handbook. We can only believe someone we know. Scripture is the inspired revelation of God about himself, together with every encouragement to trust him. All the knowledge of God that we need is set out in Scripture for us. Experience is not the Bible, but the Bible must be translated into experience. Experience means trust and trust means commitment and action.

Faith is not believing what you know is not true. Faith is believing God, whom you know is true. It is about a relationship of friendship and trust. John's Gospel is particularly a faith book. Chapter 20 ends: *"These are written that you may believe that Jesus is the Christ, the Son of God, and that by believing you may have life in his name."*

When one looks at the original Greek text of John's Gospel, it is surprising to find that the noun "faith" is never used, even though that Gospel is outstandingly the Gospel of faith. The words that are used are always "believe" and "believing." [2] The reason is that for John Christianity is an ongoing ever-present experience, not a doctrine, theory or an account of past events. He never treats faith as an attachment or static accessory but always as a living, active

[2] Greek verb *pisteuo*, never the noun *pistis*. Also never *peithomai* – to convince.

attitude of soul. John always likes the dynamic and continuous. He prefers participles like "receiving," "seeing," and "coming." Eternal life is not a deposit attached to us or held by us, but life eternally coming from God, not a something deposited with us. Whittle's fine hymn says, "Moment by moment I'm kept in his love; moment by moment I've life from above."

"Believing" is not agreeing with or assenting to a creed or doctrine. It has been said that the creed of the early church was "Jesus is Lord"; today we say, "Jesus saves." Even that modicum of truth can bring salvation. A complicated doctrine is not needed. Bible truth always comes back to God, *"trust in the Lord."* The heart of the whole business is God, Jesus. The church has often taught that to become a Christian people need to learn the catechism but the catechism can follow salvation where there is repentance and faith.

> The word of God seems dead to unbelievers but becomes alive to believers. Potent faith is not passive but active.

The word of God seems dead to unbelievers but becomes alive to believers because their experience matches it. Bible believing means looking up to Christ Jesus and saying, "Yes, Lord!" Charles Wesley's great hymn says, "All my trust on Thee is stayed." Potent faith is not passive but active.

We are told to preach the word because it reveals Christ. Then hearers can trust him. Testimony alone may create interest merely as a character study of what some special person happens to be like, that he plays the piano, does gardening, or goes to church. It is a testimony to what a man does, whereas the gospel testifies to what God does. However, when testimony declares the claims of Christ, it becomes more than an interesting fact about somebody; it becomes a challenge, with effects on others. *"Faith comes from hearing the message, and the message is heard through the word of Christ"* (Romans 10:17). We are born again by the word of God because it reveals God.

That is the genius of the Scriptures. They introduce us to God's activity of salvation. Many sacred books exist, but only one, the Bible, speaks of salvation by faith, by trust, resting one's life and eternity on God. Pagan cults and mystery religions called for commitment but promised nothing. Jupiter, Apollo, Artemis, the Olympian gods, had devotees but not "believers." No one trusted them. They did not save, care, forgive, guide, or see people through life here and hereafter. A hundred million such gods in Asia do nothing for their devotees. Which follower of any religion on earth except Christianity can say, "I'm forgiven. My sins are blotted out"?

A Christian walks with God. God is not tethered to a shrine. The living God speaks and acts; he is a person we can know. God came to Abraham as a friend, and Abraham became the friend of God, an impossible idea except when connected with the God of Abraham. The Lord comes not to judge or to treat us as worthless nobodies; he comes to open his heart and calls us *"my people."*

The main satanic ploy is not to tempt us to sin but to unbelief. Satan is anti-god and seeks to destroy trust in God. He began in the Garden of Eden, sowing seeds of disbelief in Eve's mind, *"Did God really say …?"* (Genesis 3:1). He misled and confused ancient peoples until he revealed himself to Abraham and Moses. The same satanic work goes on now *"in those who are disobedient"* (Ephesians 2:2).

The advantages of trusting in God are obvious yet many deprive themselves of them. It is a moral tragedy, not a quirk. The name of Jesus is shunned as if he were the omen of disaster. It seems almost paranoid, but it is the deceptive work of the devil. Unbelievers scorn believers without any notion of what believing is like. The Christian life is beyond the normal. Evangelism is not argument. Preaching is not lecturing, debate. It is intended to promote a state of heart, to encourage trust in God.

The word of God is a word to the deaf and the dead. In a vision Ezekiel saw a valley of dry bones. God said, *"prophesy,"* and as Ezekiel spoke, the bones "heard," life came into them, and they stood up as an army. Jesus said that the dead will hear his voice in the grave and come forth alive (John 5:25). We preach to those who are deaf and to those who are lying in spiritual graveyards of unbelief, dead to all spiritual sensitivity, entombed in leaden doubts. The word brings resurrection; the dead hear and live to walk in the sunshine of the smile of God. It happens all the time.

Faith is a common human faculty. Life does not stand still; each hour we step into uncertainty. We need faith in relationships at home or work, in machines, buildings, medicines, doctors, businesses, and organizations. We exercise judgment about who or what to trust and to what degree, almost by instinct. That ability is faith, the gift of God, like eyesight or hearing.

That faculty can be damaged by a psychiatric disorder, which is a common illness. People become depressed, mortally frightened of something, mistrusting everything. Not to believe in God may have the same unnatural cause, for universally people have always believed in some form of god.

Faith is perfect in children. Children know nothing about faith but they trust their parents and others. That is true faith. Faith does not struggle but relaxes. People become introspective, looking to see if they have faith. It is not something to see; it is what you do. We go ahead relying on the fact that God is with us. Jesus did not ask people if they had faith but he was very grieved when they were scared or anxious.

Faith is a hand. We put our confidence in a friend with a handshake. Jesus told a man with a shriveled hand, *"Stretch out your hand"* (Matthew 12:13). If our faith is "shriveled," we can do the same at his command. We choose to trust God just as we choose to trust anybody else, but the Holy Spirit will be behind it.

The Holy Spirit has come to prompt us into believing. When we exercise our faith it is by the Holy Spirit. The day of Pentecost made that difference. We are witnesses because we are believers.

Jesus taught. Taught what? He said, *"Learn from me"* (Matthew 11:29). He is the Truth. The truth sets free. The word says, *"Preach the word!"* (2 Timothy 4:2). So – do just that, remembering that Jesus is the Word.

Question

How do we grow in faith?

Do not merely listen to the word,
and so deceive yourselves.
Do what it says!

James 1:22

Epilogue

What you have read in this book is not theory from a college cloister. It is the product of many years of smelting and molding in the Holy Spirit fires of face-to-face witness for Christ.

Then ten years ago film scripts began to be written and films planned, conceived in the same mould. This two-volume book and the Full Flame Films are now being released together as originally planned. A vast amount of thought has gone into this book and a vast amount of thought and money into the Full Flame Film project. Why? From the very beginning, the intention has been to accomplish the greatest-ever effort to stimulate world evangelism.

There are thousands of gospel agencies and it is our hope that these films and books will provide new help for them all. We want them to be an injection in the right arm of the church, to invigorate and to galvanize serious and determined effort to reach everyone in the world with the message of salvation in Christ Jesus. The Full Flame Films and these two volumes are to be distributed around the globe in many languages. So far as we know, nothing of this scale has ever been undertaken before.

When it comes to evangelism, enough study is enough. You cannot learn to play the piano better by hearing more lectures about piano-playing techniques. You have to put your fingers on the keys. Evangelism is not a sit-down-and-learn topic. It is a "hands-on" activity, a demand, a challenge, a commission and a consuming passion. The old saying is that to start is half the battle. It is the start the devil hates and will block if he can, using his favorite deterrent of fear. Perfect love casts out fear; when we love the souls of men, fear flees.

The Father, the Son and the Spirit each depend on us. Salvation is their greatest work, the Father sending the Son, the Son dying and the Holy Spirit empowering mortals for immortal service. The awesome stellar infinity does not occupy the mind of God any more than the business of even one evangelist or one humble witness.

Governments are spending millions trying to detect extra-terrestrial life. If the scientists did indeed contact other sentient beings in other worlds, it does not alter the fact that God sent his Son to planet earth for the great battle with sin and death. This world is the battleground of the universe. Here the mighty arms of God bent his arrowed bow against the evil that had invaded the very cosmos. *"The reason the Son of God appeared was to destroy the devil's work"* (1 John 3:8). He has not changed his mind or slackened in zeal. For his eternal purposes his focus is on the people of this planet. God loved the world like that, practically, everything diverted to one single-minded purpose, salvation. We should make no mistake about it; it is here with our fellow mortals, that God wants us, as the agents of his omnipotence. It all depends on us.

It also depends on him, but he never fails. God has left us here to do the necessary task of making known the word of Christ. That is not his work; it is ours. It is almost frightening, but that is our responsibility. Asking God to come down supernaturally and do what we are here to do is wasting our breath. We are to save souls. Tremendous strivings over long years in prayer are made for God to move in revival and saving power. Yet he does not operate like that. God chose *"through the foolishness of preaching to save those who believe"* (1 Corinthians 1:21). He cannot act until we act. He goes when we go.

People talk about the mighty power of prayer to move God. God talks about the mighty power made accessible to us, the same power that raised Jesus from the dead (Ephesians 1:19-20). Do we

really need to persuade God to save? It is his work! So surely he
will do it without our pressing and urging him. All he waits for is
our cooperation, our willingness to do what he set us here to do.
Saving is his own work. He is the Savior. We do not beg a doctor
to doctor us, nor a footballer to play football. They do what they
do because that is what they are.

There are times when God seems to rise and invade and turn
a town over and draw many to himself. We have called such
occasional happenings "revival". But from whatever aspect or from
whatever theological position we view such events, nothing can
alter the fundamental fact that God never changes in mood, action
or power; nor is he different from one town to other or from one
country to another. Just as I am me wherever I go, God is himself
the whole world over. He is what he is and will do what he does
in every place, namely, to back every gospel witness with his full
presence and power.

God has no periphery, no stray wisps of power catching some
places rather than others. Anything that suggests otherwise must
be judged by the Word. Jacob was where God was and admitted
the next day that he had not been aware of it (Genesis 28:16). Jesus
was in a house and *"the power of the Lord was present for him to
heal"* (Luke 5:17), but nobody there was healed. He said that he
had often wanted to save Jerusalem but he did not. God's presence
is not diminished, but the Spirit can be quenched.

We do not judge the power or presence of God by human reactions. Many resist the Spirit, as Stephen accused his murderers
in Jerusalem of doing. Evangelism means just doing our duty and
leaving to God what we cannot do. Our campaigns not only bring
decisions for Christ, but we make sure each convert is counseled
and given the milk of the Word in a gift book (at the time of
writing 70 million such books have been printed). We contact
churches to look after these new Christians.

People read the thrilling stories of "revivals" and the heart cry is often "Lord, do it again!" However, God may have other plans. Who are we to dictate to him how to act? How God operated a century or two ago does not stand as a promise for today. The past is not our Bible. In the true and only Word, we read what we can expect now.

In his earthly ministry Jesus chose individuals and saved them – his way. Then he went everywhere with the disciples confirming the Word by the signs that accompanied it. That is the evangelistic formula, but it produced varied responses. In Samaria it generated great joy, in Athens great thought, in Berea great Bible searchings, in Corinth great affection for the apostle. God honored the proclamation of the gospel and multitudes turned to Christ from heathen darkness. Conversions under the apostles nowhere were characterized by prostrations, convulsions, agonies and convictions. God was pleased to save souls like that in the services of Whitfield, Wesley, the Circuit Riders of the West or the old traveling evangelists in Britain and Europe. But he saves souls anyway he likes. Salvation is his work of love and wisdom. He will cooperate absolutely with any of us when we pray, or how we pray, when we work or how we work, if our objective is the same as his – salvation.

In Africa we have seen over one million people turn to Christ in one meeting. I have also preached in a meeting attended by no more than five individuals. God's prize does not come from doing great things but from doing anything for him. That is what we are for – for him. The man Jesus said was the greatest born of women, John the Baptist, said himself that he was not fit to release the strap of Christ's sandals.

If we do nothing for God, we do nothing and we live for nothing. The awful gap exists between those doing something for him and those that do not, which is the major division between human beings. We can stand with which group we like. *"Do not merely listen to the word, and so deceive yourselves. Do what it says!"* (James 1:22).

"I urge you, brothers, in view of God's mercy, to offer your bodies as living sacrifices, holy and pleasing to God – this is your spiritual act of worship" (Romans 12:1).

Notes: _____

FULL FLAME
F I L M   S E R I E S

IGNITING A PASSION FOR THE LOST

NEW!

An 8 part film series combines modern day and biblical stories with the teachings of Reinhard Bonnke in a sweeping cinematic presentation on soul-winning.

Empower your church today with a Master Pack, complete with discussion guides, 8 DVDs, an inspirational music CD, and principles on revolutionary evangelism.

Join the battle cry for the heart of mankind. Be ignited to share your faith.

For more information,
www.fullflamemovie.com

Effective Soulwinning

THE REINHARD BONNKE
SCHOOL OF FIRE

Learn how to be an explosive soul-winner!

Get ignited and have a fire kindling your evangelistic skills with 8 easy online lessons. Through Reinhard Bonnke's proven soul-winning experience and tools for evangelism, you will gain valuable insights and learn how to bring the world's lost to Christ.

Here's what the **School of Fire** will teach you:

- ▧ The basic principles of imparting the truth about the Fire
- ▧ The truth about Salvation
- ▧ Evangelism as explained in the Bible
- ▧ How to practice global Evangelism
- ▧ How to depend on the Holy Spirit
- ▧ Proven methods for Discipleship and Follow-up

The **School of Fire** will stir a passion for lost souls in you!

Study at your own pace while our comprehensive testing ensures that you have the skills you need to be an explosive soul-winner!

Register online today at:

www.schooloffire.com

and learn how to spread the fire!

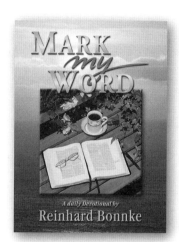

366 DEVOTIONS one for every day of the year

Mark my Word

"Mark my Word" is a carefully compiled collection of dynamic daily devotionals from the perceptive writings of Evangelist Reinhard Bonnke. Every day you will read sharp, personal, seasoned Biblical insights that have been comprehensively prepared (with thorough scriptural cross-referencing) to help you reap the full benefits from each of the life-changing applications found on every page. You will be enriched and encouraged. In this one volume you'll also discover a wealth of basic Bible background information and inspiration that you'll be able to absorb and apply at your own pace – on a daily basis.

With its simple, convenient, easy-to-read format, you can take this book anywhere and plunge in at any point – choosing to read specific indexed selections focused on a particular topic or category of interest – or read it through and use it as your personal daily devotional, daily Bible reading program, and Bible study guide. "Mark my word" will help you make the most of your Bible reading time as it strengthens your daily walk with the Lord.

418 pages • ISBN 3-935057-18-0

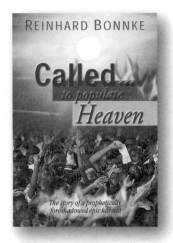

Called to populate Heaven

This is the miraculous story of how over 3.4 million Nigerians found salvation in the city of Lagos, Nigeria, during CfaN's Millennium Crusade. The crusade turned out to be the largest ever held by the organization!

DVD • Widescreen • 60 min. • ISBN 0-9758789-6-4

Raised from the Dead

This is the remarkable story of a Nigerian pastor, Daniel Ekechukwu, who was fatally injured in a car accident near the town of Onitsha, Nigeria, Africa on November 30th, 2001. During a dramatic journey to a hospital in Owerri, Nigeria, he lost all life signs and was later pronounced dead by two different medical staff in two different hospitals. The latter wrote a medical report and commissioned the corpse to the mortuary. But Daniel´s wife remembered a verse in Scripture from Hebrews 11:

"Women received their dead raised to life again."

She heard about a meeting where Evangelist Reinhard Bonnke was going to preach, and acted by bringing Daniel´s body in his coffin.
What follows is a story you will never forget.

This DVD contains the following languages:
English, German, French, Spanish, Portuguese and Russian.

DVD • 50 min. per language • ISBN 0-9758789-4-8

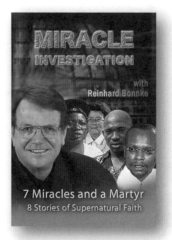

Miracle Investigation
7 Miracles & 1 Martyr

Miracle Investigation reveal the fascinating facts surrounding 8 modern-day miracles.

How did a deaf man hear once more? Can the lame walk again? Is it true a man lay dead for days on end, embalmed for burial, and then came back to life?

Join Reinhard Bonnke, a man well acquainted with the miraculous, as he explores these supernatural events.

DVD • 66 min. • English, French, German • ISBN 3-937180-07-9

The Power Channel of Intercession
3 part CD set

"Praying is big business in the heavenly kingdom. No person can ever rise higher than on their knees before God. Prayer is the wonder-gift of the grace of God and our highest natural capacity. It brings us into cooperation with Him and He with us."

Join Evangelist Bonnke as he shares an in-depth study on the subjects of prayer and intercession with some of the CfaN Team.

The teachings are also available on VHS video.

3 CDs • 150 min. • ISBN 1-933106-04-2

PRODUCTIONS
Evangelistic Resources

For ordering Reinhard Bonnke products, please visit our website

www.e-r-productions.com

We also carry a wide range of **products in other languages**,
such as German, Spanish, Portuguese, French ...

Please contact your local office for other languages:

North America & Canada

E-R Productions LLC
P.O. Box 593647
Orlando, Florida 32859
U.S.A.

Europe

E-R Productions GmbH
Postfach 60 05 95
60335 Frankfurt am Main
Germany

Asia & Australia

E-R Productions Asia Pte Ltd.
451 Joo Chiat Road
#03-05 Breezeway in Katong
Singapore 427664

Latin America

E-R Productions Ltda
Avenida Sete de Setembro
4615, 15 Andar
Batel, Curitiba – PR
80240-000
Brazil

Southern Africa

E-R Productions RSA
c/o Revival Tape and
Book Centre
P. O. Box 50015
West Beach, 7449
South Africa

CfaN CHRIST FOR ALL NATIONS

For CfaN Ministry write to:

North America

Christ for all Nations
P.O. Box 590588
Orlando, Florida 32859-0588
U.S.A.

Canada

Christ for all Nations
P.O. Box 25057
London, Ontario
N6C 6A8

Asia

Christ for all Nations
Asia/Pacific
Singapore Post Centre
Post Office
P.O. Box 418
Singapore 914014

Latin America

Christ for all Nations
Caixa Postal 10360
Curibita – PR
80.730-970
Brazil

Continental Europe

Christus für alle Nationen
Postfach 60 05 95
60335 Frankfurt am Main
Germany

United Kingdom

Christ for all Nations
250 Coombs Road
Halesowen
West Midlands, B62 8AA
United Kingdom

Australia

Christ for all Nations
Locked Bag 50
Burleigh Town
Queensland 4220
Australia

Southern Africa

Christ for all Nations
P O Box 50015
West Beach, 7449
South Africa

Please visit our website
www.cfan.org